What has been said about *Purposeful Parenting* and Jonathan & Melissa Brown

"I have had the privilege to watch and walk with Melissa and Jonathan Brown as a couple, a family and as parents. I know each of their kids, and in a beautiful and unique way they are all warm, kind, appropriately confident and spiritually engaged and relationally engaging young people. Not only do their children love and cherish their parents, they also deeply appreciate the familial bond they share. I am so grateful the Lord has them in my life."

CHAP CLARK, Pastor of St Andrew's Presbyterian Church - Newport Beach, California; author

"The Discipleship of Parenting sums up the content of this book very nicely. Both Jonathan and Melissa live out their discipleship to Christ by modeling and living it alongside their children. Words that come to mind are intentional and focused. This book on parenting puts emphasis on the intentionality of focusing on what God is up to and then continually joining God in the process of forming our children into the adults God created them to be. I highly recommend this book, not only for the content, but for the evidence I have seen in the lives of the seven children that God has entrusted Jonathan and Melissa to raise up."

TREVECCA OKHOLM, author of *Kingdom Family: Re-Envisioning God's Plan for Marriage and Family*

"We've had the privilege of knowing Jonathan and Melissa for quite a while now, and we've been hoping they would write a book since the first day we met them! We can tell you honestly that they live out the truths that they teach in this book, and their family is the better for it. Rarely do you come across children, teens, or young adults that are more respectful, joyful, kind, or generous than the Brown's are. Their God-inspired balance of giving such beautiful grace to their children while still expecting them to rise up and live life through the holiness of God is a beautiful thing to watch. I know you'll be inspired and blessed as you read this book and apply their wisdom to your own family."

JASON DUFF, pastor of The Garden Fellowship - Bermuda Dunes, California; author of *The Fundamentals of Walking With God* and *Groundwork*
CHRISTY DUFF, Women's ministry leader, speaker, mother of three; author of *Magnify*

"In Purposeful Parenting, Melissa and Jonathan have put together a marvelous gift just waiting to be unwrapped for all who have been given the stewardship of children entrusted to them by the Lord. They share from the heart how they have raised their children – things that are seemingly unknown to most parents in this present day. They include five basic ingredients essential in the foundation of your children and the culture of your family. They share stories from their own lives with their children to help in application of the essentials of parenting. And they include biblical support for all they share, demonstrating a high regard for the authority of God and His Word. Their application questions will help you in living out all that you learn. They address specific questions that you have most likely asked on your own parenting journey.

Melissa and Jonathan don't just talk about parenting, they have done it. They have parented in an amazing and powerful way. I love watching Melissa and Jonathan with their seven children. Their family literally stands out in a crowd, like a light in a dark room.

I highly recommend that you spend time reading Purposeful Parenting and you will discover nuggets of gold to apply for yourself in how to raise your children to love the Lord and follow Christ. Heaven will tell the story of the glorious ripple effect as you give them the beauty of God, His Word, and His ways."

CATHERINE MARTIN, Founder, Quiet Time Ministries; Author and Speaker

"Melissa and Jonathan's view of parenthood is a breath of fresh air in modern times, both convicting and inspiring. The greatest proof of their parenting methods are their SEVEN amazing children- kind, respectful, faithful, disciplined, vibrant, humble and phenomenally talented… whether in Division 1 basketball or symphony violin. Their children's success is not an accident, but the result of thoughtful, intentional, prayerful guidance and instruction. In this book, Melissa and Jonathon provide a window into how they have instilled identity and purpose while providing instruction, guidance and discipline. They discuss how to lead children into adulthood and how to walk alongside them at each phase of their development- physically, emotionally, relationally, spiritually. Their thoughtful hands-on approach and their probing questions will help you define what you want your own parenting to look like, and how you can join God in the work He is already doing in the lives of your own children."

KRISTIN PELINKA, MD FAAP Pediatrician, wife and mother of two

Purposeful Parenting

Freeing Parents from the Ignorance and Misinformation of the World

Jonathan & Melissa Brown

With Tatiana Brown

Lifeways for Living

While any stories in this book are true, some names and identifying information may have been changed to protect the privacy of individuals. Except for our children…their shame shall be exposed. mwahaha.

Cover photo by: Jennifer Unkrich
Cover design by: Simeon Brown

Lifeways for Living
lifeways4living.com
lifeways4living@gmail.com

"Our culture has lost its way with respect to parenting. We are a rudderless ship without a compass. We lack both a sense of direction and the capacity to direct ourselves."

- Ted Tripp, "*Shepherding a Child's Heart*"

To our children:
Simeon, Lionnel, Tatiana, Elijah,
Judah, Elyona, Joshua, and Joseph

Table of Contents

Introduction

When our oldest children strolled into their twenties, they naturally ran right into adulthood; and there was a new vigor to understand how life and relationships worked. This book arose out of one of their quests for understanding, it is the result of their questioning. They noticed differences in the perspectives, values and results of their upbringing and that of peers around them and they appreciated who they were. What's more, they wanted to know what we did and vowed to send their children to us to do it to them too. Since that was not an option, because they were raised to be able to parent their own children, they asked us "how did you raise us to be us?"

This book is to our children. To remind you of things we did as parents and to show you why we did them. You know the results since you are the results. Our desire is that you train your children in like manner and train them to train their children and so on. I guess that all the years of teaching you was the first step. Teaching you to teach is the final step. So here it is, the discipleship of parenting. Enjoy.

Perspectives

In all our years of education (combined that is over 25 years of classroom instruction starting at kindergarten) there was not one single class that taught us how to parent. Parenting used to be demonstrated to children by their parents, and from them, you were expected to learn and know how to be a parent in turn. Both of our parents did an excellent job of modeling good parenting, but we never attended a parenting class outside of the ones we taught. You would think that something that is so important to the fabric of our society would have more emphasis placed upon it within the educational and societal systems. Parenting usually ends up being a blend of actions and techniques that are highly influenced by the things an individual likes and dislikes about their upbringing, combined with a little common sense, and based on beliefs they adopted as adults.

Purposeful Parenting

There are professionals that are available to help us when it comes time for the delivery of a child (we pay these medical doctors quite handsomely), we see professionals again when the child becomes emotionally unstable, or we become emotionally unstable (and we pay the psychiatrist quite handsomely also). But is there a way, somewhere between birth and emotional instability, to direct the path of our children, and maybe even our own path, in such a way as to accomplish something great? Is it just luck? Do we just get good kids or bad kids and it's up to the luck of the draw?

We want to help you become good parents. That involves many things, much more than just getting your children to do what you want them to do. It involves much patience, much love, much compassion, much appreciation and joy in being with your children. Parenting is seeing your children, truly seeing them.

Introduction

Parenting is more than techniques. It is the development of parents and perspectives.

There are many facets to parenting, many of which we will address in mini chapters in this book. Read them, digest them, let them influence you. Begin to change your habits, your priorities and your ways. Become effective parents. Make parenting part of your answer to the questions, "What do you do?" and "Why do you do what you do?".

Parenting is a Discipleship Journey through Relationships

What is parenting? It is molding the heart of another by the transfer of knowledge and truth through what you do. It is discipleship. It is teaching your children to follow Christ by having them follow you (1 Corinthians 11:1). Deuteronomy 6 puts it beautifully:

These are the commands, decrees and laws the Lord your God directed me to teach you to observe in the land that you are crossing the

> *Jordan to possess, so that you, your children and their children after them may fear the Lord your God as long as you live by keeping all his decrees and commands that I give you, and so that you may enjoy long life. Hear, Israel, and be careful to obey so that it may go well with you and that you may increase greatly in a land flowing with milk and honey, just as the Lord, the God of your ancestors, promised you.*

The instruction here is to teach them to observe the commands so that they learn to respect God. Observing the commands is not the goal. The commands could never give life. The goal is the relationship with the giver of life. It goes on to say:

> *Hear, O Israel: The Lord our God, the Lord is one. Love the Lord your God with all your heart and with all your soul and with all your strength. These commandments that I give you today are to be on your hearts. Impress them on your children. Talk about them when you sit*

at home and when you walk along the road, when you lie down and when you get up. Tie them as symbols on your hands and bind them on your foreheads. Write them on the doorframes of your houses and on your gates.

The goal is to love God with all your heart. The method: teach them by loving God in all you do. This is discipleship. This is parenting.

Parenting is truly about relationships. It is building a sincere and genuine love relationship with your child, just as God the Father has with Jesus and desires to have with us. It is where you, by the grace of God, learn the hearts of your children and win those hearts for Jesus. It is a relationship where you come to truly know your child as you join God in forming them into who He has intended them to be. You are not forming them into your image or some ideal that you have, but simply guiding them in becoming who God has created them to be. This takes much work and time. Most of the time you invest will be in developing your own intimate relationship with Jesus; you must spend time in prayer and the Bible daily as that is where you will receive most of your spiritual insight and discernment about the hearts of your children. It is here that you will learn what they are struggling with, what their hearts needs are, and have your eyes trained to see what God is doing in and with them. On a day to day basis their giftings, aptitudes and purpose will be revealed as you remain in this place of abiding. And as you simply live one day at a time, the child's giftings will begin to blossom like a budding flower.

Get to know your child. Their heart, their gifting, their calling. You do this by spending purposeful time with them daily. By purposeful time I mean time where you are looking into their eyes talking with them, whether over a board game, reading aloud, or simply laying on the floor speaking with them. Undivided time with just them. No other distractions.Then join God in the work He's doing in forming them. Again, you are not to make them into what you think they ought to be, but guide them to what the Lord has determined they ought to be.

Melissa on the topic, "My motivation in parenting:"

My task in parenting was to give to our children the beauty of God and the beauty of His word and the beauty of His ways. I displayed this beauty through my love for them. Understanding that my children were a gift from God, given to me to raise for His glory, motivated my love for them. I knew that parenting was primarily about showing them God. That is why I moved the way I moved. We did what we did because we were called to this task of parenting by His gift of children. And these were His children that He gave me stewardship over.

Simeon's dedication cake said, "Simeon Gilkes Brown on loan from the Lord." Our children are on loan from the Lord. We are just stewards. They are His children. We were the ones chosen to steward

---

the seven children that He put in our care. So my motivation was always to raise them up in the way that God designed and desired for them to go. To guide and direct their hearts, minds and beings to understand who God is and who they are in light of who He is. I raised them to know that they belong to God.

The foundation of all our parenting was love. God defines himself as love and if God is love and I am His, I must move in that love. So everything I did with the children was done in love and with compassion. Love is what my heavenly father extended to me. He extended love, compassion, understanding, patience and discipline. His love was extended to me on the cross. His love was displayed in allowing me to be reconciled to Himself.

We teach our children that their purpose in life is to bring glory to God. Even in our discipline of our children, when they were acting in disobedience, we helped them to see that their disobedience was not accomplishing their life objective, which is to glorify God, and if they are not glorifying God, they are not fulfilling their purpose. We always brought them back to that, we would tell them, "When you are being obedient, you are inside the circle of God's protection. When you are disobedient or rebellious you walk outside of that circle. You are walking out of the protection of God that keeps you safe. So our move is to draw you back in. Discipline and correction, sometimes through spanking, is done to return you to the safety of God's covering." We did everything we did to bring our children to an understanding and a revelation of who God is in their lives, who God is in the world, and what God's plan is for them. And we taught them to submit their will to His by joining Him in the work He was doing. They did that by obeying, respecting, and honoring us because that is what He said to do.

This is the overarching perspective and view. The

purpose for which we are parenting. Why are we doing what we do? It is what we are called to, to honor and glorify God. We must point our children to the cross, to His word, and to His ways. That's the nutshell of it.

The reason behind our parenting is that we want to raise up generations who are blameless and innocent before God. We want to raise children of God who are without blemish in the midst of this crooked and twisted generation. We want our children to shine as lights in the world, we want them to hold fast to the word of life so that in the day of Christ, we may be proud that they did not run in vain. By this we will also know that we did not labor in vain. This is Philippians 2:12-18.

Your relationship with your child should be a mirror for them of their future relationship with their God. This is why it is not sufficient to say "my children do whatever I tell them not to do, so I don't tell them what to do. I just make suggestions because I know they will do the opposite". If they interact with God the way you have taught them to interact with you, they will not obey God and they will live a rebellious life toward the creator? Let the relationship and interactions that you have with your children be the same as what their interactions and relationships should be with their God. They should respond to God in respect, reverence and obedience, and you should teach them to respond to you in a like manner.

This brings us to the point of making some definitions and answering some questions: *What is effective parenting and how do I know when I have reached it?*

Effective parenting is parenting in such a way that you reach the goals that you set for your children's hearts and your children become effective parents.

(They who write the book, make the definitions.) If you define effective parenting in a different way than this, you need to hear us out. Out of the heart of the person comes all the actions and outcomes. The actions of a child cannot be the goal. The goal must be to influence the heart and the actions will follow. The goal cannot simply be to influence the heart of one generation. To influence the heart of one generation is to establish a foundation that says, "This works for me but it may not work for everyone", or "This is true for me but it may not be true for everyone." The goal must be generational. It must establish truths that are true today, tomorrow, and forever. It must establish a heart that reproduces itself. Without this, society dies.

OK that's a little dramatic, maybe society just decays into chaos.

So let's summarize,

Effective parenting is parenting in such a way as to impact the heart of a child, and to impact that heart in such a way that the child then sees

himself or herself as a reproducer of the impact.
We must learn to parent for the ages.

Questions to Ponder

Perspectives

1) Before considering the ideas of this book, how did you define parenting?

2) Do you believe that having "good kids" is just up to "the luck of the draw"? Or Is it possible to direct the path of your children?

3) What are some of the things involved in becoming "good" parents?

4) What is meant by "parenting is truly seeing your children"?

5) In desiring to become Effective Parents which of your habits, priorities, and ways might need to be changed?

Parenting is a Discipleship Journey Through Relationships.

1) How is parenting defined in this section?

Introduction

2) What is the goal in teaching your children to observe the commands & decrees of the Lord?

3) How do you learn the hearts of your children?

4) Have you personally developed an intimate relationship with Jesus through time in the Bible and prayer?

If you do not have a relationship with Jesus and would like to begin one right now, you'll find a section titled "Life" in the appendix of this book.

5) If you do have an ongoing relationship with the Lord, how might He be challenging you to grow that relationship right now?

Motivation
1) What is my relationship with my child to mirror?

2) How should I teach my children to respond in their relationship with/to God?

3) How is effective parenting defined in this book?

4) In this section we quote Proverbs 4:23. Look at that passage in a bible and write it down there.

Introduction

Chapter 1
The Basic Ingredients of Parenting - R.A.M.S.Be.

Let's think of parenting like baking bread. There are many different types of bread but most of them have the same basic ingredients: flour, water, sugar, yeast. The same basic ingredients combined with different techniques and additional elements create different flavors and textures. Your children are unique and they will require some unique treatment, but there are a group of ingredients in the parenting process that are the same across the board. These ingredients are:

1) **Respect**
2) **Authority**
3) **Modeling**
4) **Structure**
5) **Belonging**

These five make up the foundation of parenting your children and will define the culture of your family.

Fact: If you want to purposely train your children to be awesome people, you will need to know how your actions are influencing these five ingredients.

As you read through these "essentials" keep in mind the importance of always dealing with your children in much grace & compassion. We don't want to handle our children in a manner that does not rightly represent our God to them.

Respect

I once heard a story about a black military officer who served during a time when black officers in the military were very uncommon. One day, as the officer walked through the base, he came upon a group of white soldiers. All the soldiers saluted except one. It is customary in the military, when an officer is present, to salute that officer in acknowledgement and respect of that officer's rank and position. The man that failed to salute was addressed and told to salute the black officer. The man responded, "I'm not going to salute any black man." The black officer responded by removing his jacket, placing it on a bench and demanding that the soldier salute the jacket because it was the rank which he had to acknowledge, not the man. That is to say, regardless of who was wearing the jacket, the bars upon the jacket represented the man's position and that position demanded respect.

I don't want you to run your household like the military, but there is an important lesson about respect that can be learned here. Children must be taught to respect authority in general and your authority specifically. This is non-negotiable and not up to the child's consideration. This must become a, "This is the way we do it in our home," thing. This respect is not earned, it is given because of the authority of one's position. We taught our children to respect us because we are the parents, respect their older siblings because they are older, respect their elders, respect teachers and respect people in authority. We may not like the president of the United States but out of respect for his office, we do not denigrate him with our words. They may not like their teacher but they will respect them as an adult and person in charge. This means they will not talk back, verbally dishonor, or be rude to, etc. If they have an issue, they will address it civilly and at the appropriate time, or bring it to their parents to address on their behalf. It is not for the child to determine if the person is worthy of their respect.

A Disrespectful Child Self-Exalts

A child that has not learned to respect position will overestimate their own position and the value of their input and ideas. They will think they can justify rude and disobedient behavior based on the actions of others, rumors, skin color, self centeredness, external appearance, economic class, academic achievement and a host of other prejudices.

Respect in a child begins with respect for their parents. You must require your young children to respect you with their words, actions, attitudes and expressions. Remember, this respect is not due because you are right all the time but because you are the parent. To clarify, this respect is not earned and it is not demanded, it is taught. Just as a child can be taught to respond disrespectfully, you can teach your children to naturally respond with respect.

Excerpts from an interview with our 16 year old daughter, Elyona, highlighting how a child is influenced by their observation of their environment:

Growing up, I considered myself in the perfect position because I was able to watch both the mistakes of my older siblings as well as the things that they did correctly. I was able to learn from their actions while not being held to the same responsibility as them, until I came to be their age. So I was able to learn before I was thrust into young adulthood. Therefore, I always considered myself in a perfect position to observe and learn everything. That's just me, I observe things. I'm an observer and I have been ever since I was little. When I was four years old, I remember observing my family, my mother especially. I remember watching her with my dad, my older siblings and making the connections between how they acted, how they treated us, how they treated each other, and how they lived life with the God they served. I remember thinking, I want that. Ever since then, my journey has been striving to obtain what I saw and more. Naturally, if you're four years old you don't really understand everything, but when you are able to taste and see from a young age, that is just magnified and that's been magnified for me ever since I was little. I know that I have been immensely blessed because I have been able to see them and they have walked with me through some major pivotal moments in my faith. So now it is just a journey of making it personal.

I feel like this also relates to me watching my

family. My life goal as a 5 year old was to be like mommy. That was all I wanted to do. So because I had such an amazing example, and I saw her, and I heard the things she said to us, because I was the only girl in the group of boys, every little thing she said just stuck.

My mother would get into a zone about talking about how amazing God is. When we were little she would pray and I would just watch her. My personal devotions were fairly long because I watched her. It started out, "lets just be like mommy, she's in there, she wakes up early. I don't really want to wake up early. So we'll just spend a lot of time." Eventually it changed for me and became, "Oh, Oh wow, Ok so this is mine but it's not just so that I can be mommy." It went beyond that. And at first I was a little leery because as a 7 year old I thought, "Wait a minute, you're thinking of being beyond mommy, to the point when mommy isn't the goal anymore, and I didn't know if I could or should cross that boundary." But when your goal is God, that's acceptable and that's what my mom had to explain to me.

Authority

The picture of authority in a child's life boils down to, "who has the final say."

A story retold by Melissa:

One day when Simeon was about 8 months old, he ventured into the kitchen and opened the cabinet door under the sink. At 8 months, Simeon was already accustomed to responding to commands. I told him in Spanish, because he understood several Spanish commands, "Cierra la puerta, hijo." Which means, "Close the door, son." I, without thought, expected him to respond immediately because he was familiar with this command and had always responded in the past. But he did not respond. He looked at the door and looked at me and remained standing in front of the door. I looked

---

at him, surprised, and I said, "Cierra la puerta, hijo." I said it again in Spanish and he did not do it. So, giving him the benefit of the doubt, maybe his brain was not translating Spanish today, I said it in English. "Close the door, son." There was not a move to close the door. At this point, I moved to him and got down on my knees so that I was at his eye level. I said to him, "Son, close the door." He sat down on his bottom and didn't close the door. He had no intentions of moving in the direction to close the door. I sat down next to him. I don't believe in taking my children's hand and moving it to make them do what I tell them to do. I have seen parents do that. I don't do that because it had to be his will submitting to my will. So I sat down with him on the kitchen floor. I looked at the door and pointed towards the door and said, "Close the door, son." He would not close the door. I sat there stunned. I took his little hand and I spanked it, "Close the door, son." He began to cry but he did not move to close the door. I was shocked and stuck because this was the first time he had not responded to my request. I was there in the kitchen with him. He was in tears, I was now in tears because my child was being self-willed. This was our first interaction with this. We were both in tears. I was sitting on the floor, he was sitting on the floor. I put him on my lap facing the door and I was sitting with him and we were both crying and I was saying through the tears, "Son, close the door." He sat there and looked at the door and looked at me. The Spirit of God said to me, "If you lose this battle, you lose." Wow. So I took his little hand again and I smacked it a couple times and said in Spanish, close the door and I went back and forth between Spanish and English, making sure he understood, giving him the benefit of the doubt. Finally this child, through tears, picked up his own hand, and closed the door. I grabbed him and hugged him, we were both sobbing and I said, "Son that's all you had to do. That's all you had to do."

As a parent, you have authority in the life of your child. You must walk in this authority. This means you do not have to trick, lie or deceive your child to get them to respond to you. You can expect it and train them to respond. You do not have to resort to manipulation.

Authority simply identifies who has the final say.

Listen to this mother's description of her child.

> "She cannot just do what I ask but will argue first. She also has a very hard time accepting no for an answer and will keep trying to argue or negotiate.
> If you ask her to brush her teeth, she'll say "Ok, but not until I finish..."
> If you tell her to clean her room, she'll say "But first I have to..."
> If you offer to take her surfing, she's likely to say "But I wanted to skate."
> And just to test her, we'll call the sky blue just to hear her argue that it is much more of a shade of aqua."

This child has been inadvertently trained to believe that she is in charge and has the final say. To her, arguing is just the way that she is supposed to exercise her authority.

Don't be afraid to exercise authority in your child's life. This includes making decisions that you feel are best for them. You are the parent, you can choose the food that they will eat and require them to eat it. This is a good thing especially since you know what their young bodies need in order to grow strong and healthy. You can choose their clothing, all the while teaching them what is acceptable. One mom said this regarding her child:

"I let her make her own choices in things such as her own outfits. She often ends up going to her preschool wearing mismatched socks, pajamas under dresses, a shirt under or over a dress, etc."

You need to exercise your authority so that a child learns how to make these choices.

We don't let our young children listen to rap music because it is unsettling to their flitting souls and makes it harder to find peace in quiet and stillness. At the same time we enjoy gospel rap with our older children. We can do that without controversy because we have authority in our home.

We do not let our younger children watch some popular movies that our older children may watch. Authority lets you do what you know is right for your children regardless of what others do or are allowed to do. This is our home and our responsibility.

Modeling

Therefore be imitators of God, as beloved children.
Ephesians 5:1

God made children to be imitators. Deuteronomy 6:6-9 reflects how children are taught by everything we do. It says we are teaching when we sit down, when we walk, when we lie down and when we rise up. By observing us, our children learn character, good habits, values, virtue, compassion and patience. Unfortunately, they are equally good at copying our bad behaviors like addictions, tempers, lying and deceitfulness. The good news is that in order to raise good children, we just need to model good behavior. That means parenting is as much raising ourselves as it is raising our children. So whether through intentional or unintentional modeling, we need to consider our actions first. We must take an honest and exposing look at ourselves and ask, " What are the things in me, whether openly or things done in secret, that I need to address so they do not become baggage or bondage to my son or daughter?"

> When my wife became pregnant with our first child, the realization that my son would be born knowing nothing, and would learn everything from me, and would copy the things that I did, and would copy my bad behaviors best of all, humbled me. I took an honest look at my sins and pursued repentance and transformation. As I look at my children today, I see my values and understanding in them. I also see my procrastination and lack of disciplined diligence flare its ugly head on occasion.
>
> - Jonathan

The concept of modeling is easy: Be the person you want your children to be, and be consistent, because they will be the person you are.

Structure

How do I bring peace to the hearts of my children? We accomplished this by providing **discipline** and **order** in the home. This takes away the guessing game and children know what is required of them. Structure moves the responsibilities of daily living off the shoulders of the children and places them on us, the parents. They are free. They know exactly what is expected of them and do not have to figure out what to do moment by moment. There is a routine and they do not have to figure out things like what to eat when they get hungry or when they will eat. From early childhood, we taught them what to do and how to do it. When they woke up we taught them to first go to the bathroom, brush their teeth, get dressed and do devotions. We taught them HOW to do devotions. We taught them HOW to get dressed. We taught them HOW to brush their teeth and comb their hair. We taught them all the disciplines of daily living which made for a peaceful, calm, and quiet environment. Within this structure, they were free to be themselves, they did not have to figure out what to do and how to do it. That burden of responsibility was on us. The walls of structure gave them clarity of expectations so they could succeed. We provided monitoring and did not need to get frustrated with them for not doing what they were supposed to be doing.

Standing On A Ball

Provide Structure. By providing structure that does not waiver or change, your children will know what to expect and what is expected of them at all times. This is actually a strong source of security for children and creates peace in their little hearts. It is the difference between standing on a solid foundation and standing on a ball. In one, your mind does not occupy itself with standing but on succeeding in the task that is before you. In the other, you always feel like you are falling and your full attention is focused on trying to figure out what you must do next in order to keep your balance. Structure their day, from wake up time to bedtime. You can even structure some unstructured time in the day. Then stick to the structure. Consistency is an important part of structure.

I cannot overstate the importance of structure. When children have full days where they have nothing to do and can do whatever they want, it breeds discontent toward authority. They need boundaries that are very well defined. Again, this brings peace to their souls and, although they may resist it at first, be faithful and diligent to establish clearly defined lines and keep to them strictly, especially when the child is very young.

(As a parent, you may struggle with rigid structure. We encourage you to follow the scriptures that speak about self-control and discipline. They are numerous, here are a few. Proverbs 25:28, 1Corinthians 9:24-27, 2Timothy 1:7, Galatians 5:22-23, Proverbs 13:4 (I especially like the way this verse identifies the soul of the diligent as being "richly supplied")).

Rigor: Another Form of Structure in the Home

"Rigorous study develops virtue in the student. Aristotle defined virtue as the ability to act in accordance to what one knows to be right. The virtuous man (or woman) can force himself to do what he knows to be right, even when it

runs against his inclinations. The classical education continually asks a student to work against his baser inclinations (laziness, or the desire to watch another half hour of TV) in order to reach a goal — mastery of a subject." (Excerpt from *"The Well-Trained Mind."*) (Bauer & Wise, 1999)

Rigor done right is the gracious use of hard work with the specific purpose of the development of virtue. Rigor here is not akin to the discipline employed by a drill sergeant of his cadets, no, it is the employment of the mind and heart to do hard things. It is a great tool to free a child from the tyranny of wants and help them to develop the drive to push themselves beyond their comfort zone.

Structure does not mean you exclude the need for laughter, joy & freedom. Structure and discipline opens the door to be free.

Structure is not something to master us but is a gift to assist us. We are to master it. A friend from church and I were having a conversation about discipline in our homes. Structure and discipline was becoming a god in her life. She found herself stressed to meet the structure and discipline requirements that she set up in her home. Instead of structure serving her, she was serving it. She shared that God revealed to her that discipline was not to control us, but that we were to master it and use it to benefit our lives. It is a gift given to us by God. When we employ this gift we should find that we have time to do things that we would otherwise be too busy to do.

Belonging

Children need to know WHOSE they are. Who do I belong to? Who cares for me? Who has my back? Give a child a strong sense of belonging and they will ooze with confidence and surety for life. The established platform of a strong sense of identity creates a stable path from which to take on life's questions and struggles.

By God's design, children find grounding in life through identity in whose they are. Identity is first established through a healthy connection with parents and family. Parents serve to paint the bigger picture by directing the child to the understanding of their identity in Christ. We teach them through constant reminders that God has blessed them with every spiritual blessing, chosen and adopted them so that they stand holy and blameless before him, forgiven them and loved them with a never ending love, promised to never leave them or forsake them, created them and made them to His true definition of beauty, called them, gifted them and made them for good works that he has planned for them. They were made for His glory and in His glory they find their greatest satisfaction.

Questions to ponder

1) What are the 5 basic ingredients that will define the culture of your family?

2) What important lesson about respect can be learned from the story about the white soldier refusing to salute the black officer?

3) What do you think will be most difficult in expecting/ requiring this kind of respect from your children?

4) What types of atmosphere does structure bring?

5) Why is a strong sense of belonging essential to children?

Chapter 2
Lies

When building a foundation it is important to first prepare the groundwork, and that means removing debris that is corrupt to the edifice that you are trying to build. Addressing lies that we tend to believe as parents is a very important task to take on. Since perspective plays such an important role in parenting, we will tackle lies at the offset.

Lie #1:

"You might find parenting unfulfilling. In fact, I would argue that parenting is not completely fulfilling for anyone—nor should it be. Our children's lives cannot and should not consume our own (much as they might devour our time and attention). Our children are not and should not be viewed as extensions of ourselves." **(Oganowski, 2017)**

Lies

There is a popular belief that children and child rearing gets in the way of fulfilling pursuits. Some would say, "I believe that somehow I should be able to parent children and still find my satisfaction in the same places that I found it before I was a parent." Then there is the thought, "I should be able to have children and not change my lifestyle."

Parenting is a life changer.

To have children and to not understand this is to live a life that will greatly frustrate your children and yourself. When you choose to have children, parenting must become what you do. It should influence every decision and every activity from the point of conception until death, and although it should not dictate every activity, it should be a constant consideration. Think about it, parenting is giving up your life to give someone else life. Friends, that is the gospel. Parenting is a visual representation to the world of the gospel of Jesus Christ. Your children are your disciples, your sacrifice is your cross, this new life and relationship with your own children is your great joy. That is parenting. It is a different stage of life that offers a host of new experiences to be enjoyed. Many things influence our decisions, it has always been and will always be that way. When you become a parent, what influences your decision must be responses toward the goals you have for influencing the heart, life and character of another person, namely your child. That is not a depressing thought. That is a great thing. Unless of course you are a selfish person. At which point my advice would be, deal with your selfishness and don't settle with it.

Truth #1:

The task of parenting is a gift from God. It transforms us and makes us better people. Enter into the joy of parenting knowing that you will be changed as you give yourself to the benefit of another.

Lie #2:

"As parents we need to train our children to be independent people. Our job is to get them to be

independent citizens that don't need anyone to survive and become successful."

The truth is, this lie began in the garden of Eden when the serpent tempted Eve to act independently of the instruction she was given by God. The deception is to do your own thing, do what seems and feels right to you. God's instruction is wise and it does not develop a young person to independence but quite the opposite, it develops them to dependence. The kind of dependence that builds community and fosters relationships. We are stronger together. We are better together. We each bring gifts, and those gifts used in harmony are like the parts of a body working together to accomplish a task. Independence requires me to have all the gifts and operate effectively with all of them. We are not trying to develop independent people in our children. We're trying to develop the gifts that our children have and show them how to live in community and share their gift with the world.

Truth #2:

We need to teach our children to be dependent on God and to live in community and family by contributing their gifts and receiving the gifting of others.

Lie #3:

"Children will rebel."

I don't know why but in parenting the worst case scenario is often considered the default normal. This is one of those times. It is true that some children will be rebellious. It is equally true that you can parent your child in such a way that destroys that rebellious nature in its infancy. Rebellion is not the inevitable path of the teenager or preteen, it is an optional character trait that a child may choose when growing up. As parents, we can provide fertile ground for this trait to grow, or we can starve it and pluck it like a weed at the first sign of its presence. To do this you must know what things rebellion feeds on. You must know what rebellion looks like when it is first a groundbreaking seedling. You must respond to rebellion with love, training and confrontation that is aggressive, unafraid, unwavering and at times may feel unconventional. Know that rebellion in your child is not an unavoidable destination on your road map of parenting. Know also that by training the rebellion out of a child you bring that child to great peace in his or her soul.

A rebellious child is manipulative by nature. He is often insecure because he feels that any sliver of peace there is will disappear the moment he acts out. Nothing in his little world is as it seems because he can, in a very real way, influence and control all things around him by his rebellion. It is a horrible feeling for a child. It is like living on an active volcano. Anything you build today may be destroyed tomorrow and the ground is always shaking with anger. There is no solid foundation on which to rest. Rebellion in a child must be destroyed, for the sake of peace within the heart of your child.

Rebellion is often the outburst of a child that feels unsafe. For some reason the child does not feel taken care of or attended to; they feel that the people in their life are untrustworthy, so they must take matters into their own hands. This is fear in the heart of a child. Your child needs an environment of consistent structure, security, peace and joy all wrapped in love.

Respect and submission to parents must always be lovingly required from the child, as this brings a sort of safety and peace into their heart. A lack of safety and peace may be the very reason the child is rebelling. Boundaries and expectations also contribute to safety, security and peace.

Your child may not be able to voice any of these thoughts or emotions, they may not be able to identify why they react to you or to situations the way they do, sometimes you may not be the problem at all. The lashing out you are seeing may simply be coming from insecurities and uncertainty that dwells within the child. As a child begins to go through the life changing transformation of moving from child to adult, there are many physiological changes occurring. In the midst of this a young person may begin to question everything he has always loved, adored and enjoyed. That hobby he always poured himself over, now he wants nothing to do with it. Those relationships that were special to him are now annoying and frustrating. That lifelong dream now seems foolish and a waste of time. It is vital, as your child goes through this stage, that you do not allow their emotions to dictate value and priorities. Stay the course and stay on track. Be led and lead with what you know and not with what your child feels today. This is an important time to direct your young teen and not be directed by them.

At about 15 years old, our first born hit what we now call The Fog. It was quite challenging. Although he had always been a strong willed child, he was also a child that was quite willing to submit to the firm and loving authority of his parents. At this stage in his life he rebelled against things that he knew to be right and true, and began entertaining lies as if they were true. As parents, we had to continually remind him of truth: we reminded him whose he was and why he was created, we reminded him that no one loved him as much as his parents, and that no one's love would ever compare to the love that we had demonstrated everyday of his life from nursing and changing dirty diapers to driving him to basketball practice. This was a long and trying stage in his life but not the norm. Normal for our children and for your children is what you establish as the foundational truths that are unwaveringly solid:

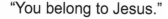

"You belong to Jesus."

"You were created for His glory."

"We love you and will act out of that love to see the character of Christ, and love for Christ developed in you."

Truth #3:

Some children will be rebellious but you can destroy the rebellious nature in its infancy by parenting your child.

Lie #4:

"If I am strict, I will push my child to rebel."
As parents, our task is like that of a gardener and this particular lie is equivalent to saying, "If you water the garden, you will make the weeds grow."

It is true that watering the garden will make the weeds grow, but the solution to the growth of weeds is not to stop watering since water is necessary for the growth of flowers also. The water does not bring about the presence of the weeds, the seeds of the weeds had to exist in the soil prior to the water. There is a proverb that says, "Folly is bound up in the heart of a child." Providing "strict" constraints for your child to operate and live in, does not cause them to rebel. Remember, it is your wisely defined structure that will make your child feel safe and confident. For some, these confines may cause the foolish rebellion that is already present in the heart to manifest itself. The solution to this revelation of ugly in the heart of a child is not to stop requiring strict boundaries of the child, but to pluck the ugliness and replace it with beauty.

Purposeful Parenting

We are always creating a better, more fertile soil that has fewer and fewer weed seeds because we pull the weeds as we see them. We are creating a more beautiful garden by planting beauty that assists in the job of making this garden less friendly to the growth of weeds.

Your child begins as an empty garden, just dirt that is littered with seeds of beautiful things and some seeds of weeds. As you nurture and water your garden everything that is there begins to grow, and yes, the weeds seem to grow faster than the beauty; thus, the gardener. With skill you will nurture your garden from the soil up, you will add beauty that was not already present in your garden, and develop harmony in your selection of beauty. You will anticipate the winds of time and place safety and security in your garden, you will be there when your garden is invaded by pests and not let them destroy it. You will do things like prune and cut back your garden at the height of its beauty so that your garden does not get too full of itself and end up smothering itself. All these things and more are accomplished by a gardener that has understanding and is intentional.

Doesn't just the thought of such a task and such a place bring a peaceful sigh and a desire to be there? There are joys of parenting. You will sit in your garden and enjoy the beauty that you have worked toward. Even if today it's just dirt littered with seeds.

Truth #4:

Your child's rebellion is a heart issue that must be dealt with accordingly. It is not a consequence of wisely established restrictions. These develop safety and confidence in your child.

Did you know that it is possible to incite someone to anger?

We have the ability to use our words and actions to stimulate a reaction in others. The Bible instructs fathers specifically to take care and not provoke their children.

> *Fathers, do not provoke your children, lest they become discouraged.*
> Colossians 3:21

This is such a simple admonition and it feels like it should be an obvious one. But in truth, men need to make a conscious effort to honor God in this area. We tend to do things that we know will aggravate those we love.

"Every time I leave my clothes on the bed she gets angry like I have done some big thing."

Have you heard a statement like that, or said a

statement like that? Well my response to this observation is, "Have you ever considered not leaving your clothes on the bed?" We call this, "Using what you know in order to be a blessing." If you know leaving your clothes on the bed will provoke anger and frustration, don't leave your clothes on the bed. This is especially wise wisdom to apply in your marriage.

Ephesians 6:4 says,

> *Fathers, do not exasperate your children; instead bring them up in the training and instruction of the Lord.*

We should exercise care in the implementation of actions, words, rules, responses and expectations as they could be the cause of irritation and frustration. The solution is training and instruction. That means purposeful consideration of the reason behind our responses and the goals we hope to achieve by them. As a father I cannot just give a cannot respond before the request is fully formed. I cannot respond to the meaning of the words without considering the intent, desire and needs of the heart. I cannot exasperate my children with actions that did not take into consideration the fact that in all I do I am helping my children see and

Lie #5:

"Spanking is child abuse and it does not work. It develops children that are more likely to lie, deceive and exhibit aggressive behavior."

This is a tough one to respond to only because of all the varying definitions of spanking. So to simplify the matter I will later define and explain what we mean by "spanking." With that promise in place, and before you jump ahead and read the spanking chapter, know that spanking done appropriately is a great tool for training the heart of a child. It is a loving response and trains a child to know love and teaches them how to display it. It develops a stronger relational bond between parent and child, in those incidents when it is needed, and it helps your child make right decisions for the long term. To many people this seems to be the opposite of their experience or expectation, I recommend and encourage them to read the section on spanking before they spank. Learn to use spanking, get your spanking training, because if you spare the rod you will spoil the child and if you use the rod you will save his soul. Also, if you misuse the rod, it is child abuse.

Truth #5:

Spanking done appropriately will bring peace to the heart and mind of your child, it will motivate them to stay on the right track.

Lie #6:

"Don't expect to always get along with your child. They will naturally not like you at some point and there will be a personality struggle between the two of you for much of their childhood."

Purposeful Parenting

Did you know that what you believe will shine through and influence what you do? This is especially true in regard to aspects of parenting because your body responds in anticipation of what the mind believes to be true. If you think the pot on the stove is hot you will treat it accordingly, even if in fact it is not hot. And there is nothing wrong with that. What you believe influences how you respond.

In parenting, a very impressionable young mind is receiving signals from your actions and forms its own belief system. Children receive cues and develop understanding of a situation from the way a parent responds. This means that we train our children by how we act and react. We teach our child to be afraid of a cockroach by being afraid of a cockroach. Would you like to guess what would happen if you walked up to the roach, picked it up with your hand and carried it outside and released it? My guess is that one day you would find a shoe box in your child's room with roaches that he claimed as pets.

Lies

The beauty here is that you have the ability to form your child's perspectives by simply changing your own. Your beliefs and perspectives influence your actions, your actions and reactions influence your child's beliefs and perspectives, your child's beliefs and perspectives influence their actions. What you believe about your child will likely be what your child will do because the steps and actions that you display toward that child will in fact nurture the very actions you don't want, but expect to occur. That means this lie is a self fulfilling prophecy. If you believe it, expect that it will be true in your case. If you do not want this to be true in your child's heart, don't believe it in your heart.

What would happen if you expected to always get along with your child, even in the tough disciplinary times?

Think about it. If something gets in your eye, it is normal to try to get it out. It is not normal to ignore the fact that something is in your eye. Yet an adult can be taught to be extremely comfortable putting a contact lens in their eye, even though touching the eyeball is against the body's comfort zone. They can be made accustomed to walking around all day with something in their eye without a thought, as if it is natural and normal.

In a similar way, a child's definition of normality is highly influenced by the parents definition of normality. They will define normal by how we define normal. The children in our family will one day get married, and when they do they will expect to be married to that person until one of them dies. Divorce in our household is not considered normal, so our children will not get married and think that they will eventually or might eventually get divorced. A divorce would be shocking because it is not normal in our household. This is true in spite of the fact that national statistics give a high probability of divorce. Even the fact that the divorce rates of their aunts and uncles are extremely high does not change their parent influenced view of what is normal.

Lies

Take as an example the car seat. If a parent thinks that a child hates being in the car seat, a crying child on the drive will be attributed to the child being in the car seat. If you believe your child loves the car seat because he is snuggled tight and can see and sleep and he knows that it will lead to the calming hum and motion of a drive, when that child begins to cry on the drive, you will attribute it to a wet diaper or something poking him in the back or hunger or sleepiness or perhaps he wants to look at me and can't see me. There is a good chance that what you believe will eventually become the very motivation of the child. Believe what you want to be true and begin to respond and react in anticipation of that truth. You just must believe it and you will be amazed at what happens, especially when it comes to the actions and attitudes your child will have in the future.

We think parents would communicate differently if they considered their words to be more like self fulfilling prophecies.
"My child is going through the terrible twos."

"My child hates math."

"He doesn't like school."

"When he is a teenager he won't want to hang out with his parents anymore."

"We talk about a lot of things, but no one tells their parents everything."

"He needs his privacy."

"No one wants to have a parent hanging around."

"I can't make him be kind to his sister."

"He is not comfortable around Mexicans."

"He would be bored in the adult church."

All these statements produce a fruit that you do not want growing in your children.

There is a cynicism in our culture regarding children. When a mom gets pregnant with her first born she is told she can say goodbye to a good night's sleep once the baby is born. When the baby is born the mom is told that things will only get worse when the child reaches the "terrible twos." After navigating the second year of her child's life, the mom is further disenchanted by foretellings of the dreaded teenage years. The only good thing for the young couple to anticipate is when the child turns 18 and moves out. The overall view of children is that they are a nuisance and inconvenience at every stage. It is so important to nurture and protect a right perspective. That pregnant mom will bring a precious new life into this world and get to pour all her love into her sweet infant. As the child grows the child will grow to love your loves and like your likes. Your child will be a sponge to absorb all that you put before them, and as they move into the teen years they will need your wisdom and strength to teach them to navigate unfamiliar waters. And when they become adults they will look to you to help reproduce their love in their children as they now learn to love a child like you loved them.

Practice speaking things that you want to be true, speak them so often that you believe them. Your child will mimic the beliefs that they see in you.

Truth #6:

Your child will live out and become the things you believe about them.

Lie #7:

"I want my child to be able to speak their opinions and share openly."

This is a very good goal. This is not a lie at all. Actually the lie hides in how we train our children to do this. The lie: Let your child speak their opinion and share openly from the moment they are able and whenever they want. As adults we shouldn't speak our opinions whenever and wherever we feel. There is a deference or respect that must always be in mind when we are expressing ourselves. Our children spend a great amount of time learning to respect with their words, eyes, facial expressions, sounds, reactions and even thoughts. This is the lesson that begins as soon as they are able. Not self expression, but how to properly express oneself.

Truth #7:

We must teach our children to properly and appropriately express their thoughts, opinions and ideas.

The lie list goes on and on. We will not address more lies here but I will give you more lies to look out for:

- Children don't want to be with their parents.
- You must force your child to get over separation anxiety early.
- Children are a bother and a burden
- Parenting is a thankless job
- I must kick them out at age 18 and they must learn to make it on their own.

The Effect of Believing the Lie

What you believe will direct your parenting. We do not want to base our parenting on the opinions of men, the culture or the latest trend, instead we want to base our thoughts and actions on design and the designer. We need to move with intention.

Design

God made us to be sponges of demonstrated and expected behavior. This is most true when we are young and this is why our young years are formative. Children are, by design, observers, discerners of actions, replicators and interpreters. They will naturally and without thought read body language, voice inflection and your choice of words to determine identity, self worth, value, priorities and expectations. This is why biblical instruction in training children involves a heavy component of considering our words and actions when we are sitting around, walking by the way or otherwise going through our day (see Deuteronomy 6). Children see and learn from the actions and words that flow out of us when we are not thinking but just living. Those actions are the fruit of our beliefs. We are molded by what we believe and we mold our children by how our beliefs are lived out. There is a cycle. Our beliefs direct our actions, our actions establish our children's beliefs, and what our children believe directs their actions.

If you believe your child to be extremely smart, you will assume that his bad grade reflects the inability of the teachers to teach genius. Your child will believe that they can elevate beyond the established knowledge of the day. They will grow to contribute innovative, new and creative ideas to make an impact on the world. What you believe directs your actions, which impacts your child's beliefs, which directs your child's actions.

What we believe directs our every move. What we believe will shape our children. If we want to become better, more effective, parents, we must purposely address our beliefs.

The Battle of our Beliefs

The battle of our beliefs is the process of taking every thought captive. But the battle is won as we consider only one belief and become aligned to it in all our life and thoughts. That belief is the very core of our existence. It is our decision to trust Jesus with our life and follow Him. This decision acknowledges the intervention of that which is supernatural into the realm of the natural. It yields to the sovereignty of the omniscient God. This is a game changer. We can, by this one act of trust, be transformed in our very minds as we pursue intimately this relationship. And parenting is perfected as we are learning to love Jesus more. Do you love Jesus?

Questions to Ponder

1) What is Lie #1?

2) Is Lie #1 a lie that you believe or have fallen prey to?

3) Has Truth #1 produced fruit in your parenting?

4) Is there a problem with teaching your children to be independent people? If so, what is it?

5) How are you to respond to budding rebellion in a child?

6) True or False: rebellion in a child is an unavoidable part of growing up.

7) What are some of the insecurities that often lead to rebellion in a child?

8) How do you direct a child who is in the midst of rebellion?

9) What is the truth in spanking?

10) How can you form your child's perspectives?

11) What is the Belief Cycle?

Lies

Chapter 3
Train Up a Child

The Bible says to train up a child in the way that they should go. Let's talk about training up a child. ^This is the most important chapter in the book because if you master this chapter everything else we discuss will be an addendum. It is important that you train your children. You cannot just expect them to know what to do when you tell them to do something. You cannot expect them to know what is right and what is wrong. You must train them.

Train Your Children

Don't assume that your children intuitively know and understand what it is you want from them without expressly telling them. If they seem to be ignoring your direction, ask questions to gain insight as to their level of understanding, then train them with clear instruction.

How Do I Train My Child?

When I train my toddler son to respond to the
command, "Come here," I say to him,

"Come here Simeon."

He just looks at me.

I motion and say, "Come to mommy. You come here."

I point to where he is, then to where he should end
up.

"When mommy says come here, you are to leave
wherever you are and come to this spot near
mommy."

We then practice the proper response a few times and
the child receives lots of praise and acknowledgement
for doing it correctly. This time of instruction, repetition
and encouragement serves to engrain the proper
response in my son's heart and mind. It also clarifies
for him the action that would be pleasing to his
parents when he is told to "come here."

By going through this process when you introduce
your toddler to a new command, you are training them
to know, and properly respond to, what is expected of

them. Your child will learn to respond respectfully and will know this as the only possible response to this request. You won't have to correct a future response like, "What" or "I'm busy, what do you want" or ignoring the request completely.

This is how a child is trained to know and do what is expected of them. There is no ambiguity that would cause him to be unclear about what he is to do. There is no worry that comes from unexpected expectations. There is peace in his little world because he understands how to move safely and peacefully within it.

Resist the temptation to assume your child knows what you mean or what they are supposed to do.

If you did not take the time to teach and explain to them what you mean and what you want, where were they supposed to learn it? Teach everything. Leave nothing to chance or interpretation.

Also train attitudes. Facial expressions, words spoken under their breath, stomping feet or other displays of frustration, should all be addressed in a training moment before it is addressed in a moment of discipline. You can and should train your child's proper reactions. Don't ignore your child's humph or rolling of the eyes. Teach them that these are not an acceptable response to a request or instruction from mommy or daddy. Then teach them how to respond. Teach them the words to say, "yes mommy," and the actions to take, "look at me when you speak."

Think and Do:

Take a moment to consider bad attitudes and reactions that your children have that you have not taken the time to train out of them. Identifying this behavior is the first step to being able to address and reverse it. You must explain to your child that these actions and behaviors are not glorifying to God, and then show them what the proper, God-glorifying action or response would be, and practice it.

The Eternal Perspective

Though it is important to teach our children right actions, it is more important to teach them why those actions are right. The "why" is the eternal perspective and is the basis for how we develop the character and heart of our children. Without an eternal perspective as your "why," any action can be justified. Without an eternal perspective, anyone can argue that anything is right. Without an eternal perspective, there is no absolute right and right is left to the definition of each individual.

I cannot just teach my children, "You cannot fight with your brother." I must also teach them that fighting with your brother does not rightly represent God before the world. I must teach them that we are to be a reflection of God to everyone. The Bible says that they will know that you are my disciples by your love for one another. I must teach them that if siblings fight each other, they fail to realize their purpose in life. Their life purpose is to glorify God. Thus, the eternal perspective is the driving force behind all we do and teach.

We taught our children through an eternal perspective. Through this they learned the priority of humility, honesty, service and other important traits. First we demonstrated life lived in light of God's values: they saw self control, goodness and gentleness demonstrated in our interactions with each other. We also taught them through the Word of God. With the Bible we trained them in the things of God and taught our children scripture as the basis of our beliefs. From John 14 and John 8, we taught our children not to lie because Jesus is the truth and Satan is the father of lies. We used a lot of scripture to teach them God's way of living. They learned how to act and interact and how to respond to us through scriptures like,

Children, obey your parents in everything, for this pleases the Lord.
Colossians 3:20.

All things were taught by example and by the Word of God.

Prayer

Additionally, we prayed for our children daily, even when they were in the womb. We prayed that their hearts would desire the things of God. We prayed for them to live for God in a way that would be honoring to Him. We prayed that they would long after Him. We prayed for their spouses long before they had a thought of marriage. We believe that the majority of our parenting was accomplished through prayer; we prayed over them and prayed with them and had them pray. Prayer established something in our household and in the hearts and minds of our children, it made the ground fertile for the ways of God to grow deep roots. Pray daily and pray early.

We talked about the things of God to and with our children. We did daily devotions and sometimes weekly devotions with them. From an early age we taught them to do their own personal devotions. We read the Word of God often, we prayed often, we gathered with the people of God often. The Lord was everything to us. Everything we did was out of the intimacy of relationship with God. Everything we did with our children was done from the eternal perspective. We did not discipline, we did not train, we did not homeschool, we did not do anything apart from what we believe the Lord to be telling us to do with them.

Training your child is ongoing, daily, moment by moment activity to the glory of God. Parenting is discipleship in godly character that is defined by the word of God. It is discipling in loving God and loving your neighbors (and your neighbors start with your parents and siblings then extend out to your neighborhood, friends, teachers, classmates and beyond). Parenting is teaching children to be obedient to God and thereby obedient to their parents. It is teaching children to be self controlled and alert. It is teaching our children to be self-governing. We must teach our children to govern their own hearts and thoughts and attitudes. We must be careful because it is possible to have well behaved children who don't know Christ or walk in His ways. We need to be careful because we want to raise children who take no confidence in the flesh but boast in Christ Jesus. This kind of training takes a lot of time and energy because you have to train the heart.

Give your child an eternal perspective:

I read about a man who was unable to help his wife shovel the snow because of a recent injury to his back. The man asked his son to go out and help the mom shovel the snow. The son responded that he did not want to go outside because he was hungry and waiting for the dad to finish making breakfast, and it was cold. He did not want to go out into the cold. The son was not going to go out and help his mom shovel the snow. The dad reasoned with his son by talking to him about community and love and told the boy that his mother was displaying love by going out and shoveling the snow. He ended with the leading questions,

---

"Don't you want to do this for your mom?"

"Don't you think your mom is hungry? "

"Don't you think your mom is cold?"

"Shouldn't you consider her?"

The son stomped off to his room and slammed the door. The dad did no more and left the situation like that. Several minutes later the son emerged from his room with his snow boots on and went outside and helped his mom.

The dad got the result he was initially after but this is not successful parenting. He did not disciple the heart of the child. He did not address the heart issues which are infinitely more important than snow removal. This son needs to know that he exists to glorify God. He needs to know that he did not consider the needs of his mother and father above his own and in doing so revealed his selfish and self-centered heart. He needs to know that the stomping and door slamming revealed an angry heart attitude. These are heart issues that are not pleasing to God. The son needs to know that Jesus gives us the power to change bad heart attitudes and he needs to repent and ask Jesus to help him have a God pleasing heart attitude. The snow shoveling incident was an opportunity for the dad to see and address the heart issues of his son. It was a teaching and training opportunity to show the power and sufficiency of the glory of God. It was an opportunity to rout out attitudes and perspectives that would otherwise fester, grow and develop a stronghold in the son's life. It was an opportunity to pray with his son.

This father did not show his son an eternal perspective. The motivation for right action was to be nice to his mom because she is being nice to you. What about the child that has a mean or uncaring mom? He is then justified to be unkind to the mom following this logic. We must teach our children to live to please God.

Questions to Ponder

1) Have you instructed your children well? Or have you left it to chance?

2) Think about the actions, reactions, and behaviors of your children that are not God-glorifying. How will you implement what you learned in this chapter to address these behaviors and institute change?

3) Do you regularly pray for and with your child, not just when there is a problem?

4) Is the goal simply to get your child to do what you want?

Chapter 4
Goals

Critical Thinking

God has designed children to be able to handle certain things at certain ages. In this day and age we try to push children to academic heights too early. This is for our good, our pleasure, to make us feel good that our children are doing critical thinking at an early age. But this does not fall in line with what God has done.

We acknowledge that puberty is a time that God works to transform a child into an adult. We also see, according to the classical approach of education, that this is the time the child enters the logic stage, which occurs around the middle school years, and children start asking "Why?". This is when children start thinking critically. This is when you should present questions and let them think through it.

Goals

Younger children are in the grammar stage. In this stage children respond to instructions. It is the stage of facts and memory, not logic and questioning. In the 2nd grade, 3rd grade and 4th grade, the "Why" of obedience is simply because mommy said so or because God said so. Parents often try to take younger children to the logic stage too soon. Often this is done by posing every decision to the child rather than giving direction. "Do you want corn or carrots?" "What do you want to wear today?" "Do you want to clean the kitchen now or later?" The grammar stage is the time to build good habits through repetition, structure and consistency, it is not the time to engage the child in making their own decisions. That time will come, don't move the child along too early or the result will be a self willed, rebellious, arrogant child who presumes to question your every move and decision.

Younger Children Must Be Guided and Led

They should not be left to themselves. Our job as parents is to give them a firm foundation upon which to stand because the time will come for them to make decisions and choices on their own. If we do not provide the grounding from which they can make good decisions; if we choose not to influence them in an attempt to let them make their own choices and be their own person, they will absorb the guiding influence of someone else. They will make decisions based upon the foundation provided to them by another. Do not be afraid to parent! You bless your child by providing the wisdom of your experience, the advantage of history, and the benefit of all that is to be learned from the Bible as the basis for them to begin making decisions. Don't force them to start without your wisdom and lose the benefit of all that God has taught you. There is a time to build a firm foundation. From this foundation they will make good decisions and choices.

Goals

As our children progress through the stages of childhood our goals in parenting do not need to change, but the methods we employ to reach them do. Our goals in parenting need to line up with what God is doing in our children. To do this we need to know what He is doing with them as they grow and develop.

What is your goal/objective/purpose in parenting? Why are you doing what you are doing with your children?

Many parents don't realize that their parenting is based primarily on the opinions of others (meaning, they do what they do to impress others). Other parents are simply dealing with issues as they arise without any real objective, except perhaps to get the child to stop whatever behavior is disrupting the peace or causing a problem.

Just as an effective company has vision and purpose driving its decisions, effective parenting must have goals that lead to purpose and drive the very framework of the family. Goals establish priorities and help in making day to day decisions.

By today's standards, we have a large family, and we are often asked, "How do you do it?" By this people mean "how do we raise so many children when raising children is such a difficult task because they require so much of us and don't contribute to making this task easier?". But people do grand things every day. It may be spending most of your waking hours working a job or two and still finding time to invest in yourself or others, it may be entertaining guests every week, or volunteering time to help others, or affording adult toys and spending the time to enjoy them. It may be remodeling a home while living in it, or contending with city traffic every time you leave the house. It may be attending to the needs of chickens, dogs, and cats, or getting an advanced education. The common thread is that we all have something that we have

determined we would do and our priorities support
that goal.

As parents, raising your children must be *one* of your
priorities. It should *not* be the top priority.
Relationships, like your relationship with God and with
your spouse, should take precedence, but these
relationships are in harmony with raising your children
well. Our parenting goals must align with how we
define raising our children well.

A Sound Goal for Parenting:
To raise our children to know and love God through
Jesus by the training of their hearts and minds. To
raise godly generations that live for the glory of God

Goals Speak to "Why"

This goal is so deep in philosophy that it spans and
speaks into nearly every aspect of an adults daily life.
There is so much biblical wisdom on this topic that we
can learn new things everyday. This goal speaks to
multiple topics including diet, health, how to pursue

and prioritize education, giftings, music and art, video games, what kind of car to buy, the use of free time, movies to watch, discipline, chores, clothing to wear and the list goes on. Most importantly it speaks to the "why" of these situations. The goal does not make your decisions for you, but it provides the "why" or the groundwork upon which you can make decisions. For example, there is no one perfect way to educate all children: home school, private school, public school, boarding school, charter school, but the way you choose should contribute to the goals you have in raising your children and not be detrimental to those goals. Your goals in raising your children should be why you choose the method of education that you choose.

We all make our decisions based on goals, we just do not always formally state our goals. When I quit that job and took another job was it because it paid more? My goal is financial. Was it because it allowed me to spend more time at home? My goal may be family time. Was it because the last boss was too stressful and this one isn't? My goal may be my health. Was it because this job offers more advancement opportunities? My goal may be a career or to provide better. Was it because this job is overseas? My goal may be experiences. Goals drive us. We need to purposely and knowingly drive our goals.

Independence

Independence should not be one of our goals for our children as they mature. We are not raising our children to be independent or to not need anyone else. Certainly we desire for our children to be strong, healthy, functioning individuals in society, but I encourage you to reconsider our calling as Christians. Our Christian calling is not one of independence but one of total dependence upon our God and mutual interdependence upon one another.

Stages of Development

Early Childhood Through Elementary Stage

Primary years goal:

Purposeful Parenting

Setting down a solid foundation of who we are in Christ as His children. Securing identity & objective.

When our children are in the elementary stage we are simply giving them information. They were created by God to absorb information. In the first few years of our children's lives their growth is exponential, both physically and mentally; they learn to turn over, sit up, crawl, pull themselves up and walk, not to mention, communicate, in a matter of months! It truly is amazing. Things slow down just a bit after the first year, but they are still absorbing a tremendous amount of information over the next few years. This is the time to begin building a strong foundation. As Christian parents, our main objective should be to define for our children not WHO they are, but WHOSE they are. We do this in our family by teaching our children through these simple catechisms.

What is a Catechism?

A Catechism is a series of fixed questions and answers used to teach a summary of principles.

- Who made you?
- Who made all things?
- Why did God create you and all things?
- How do you glorify God?

Answers:
- God made me.
- God made all things.
- For His own glory!
- By loving Him and keeping His commands.

At this point we are not going into any deep conversations with our children, they are simply receiving information based on the word of God. This information will serve to create a strong foundation that will be drawn upon later in their development.

Rote memory of catechisms has served us, and historically, generations of believers, well during this stage. We have used "A Catechism for Boys and Girls" found in the back of the book "*Truth and Grace Memory Book, Book 1*," edited by Thomas Ascol. Practice reciting the questions daily and teaching your child to answer the questions exactly. Add a new question weekly and keep learning.

How we use catechisms:

When one of our youngest boys responds to his brother in a way that is not loving, we pull him aside and have a talk with him.

"Son, who made you?"

"God made me."

"Why did he make you?"

"To glorify Him"

"How do you glorify Him?"

"By loving Him in keeping his commands."

"What is His greatest command?'

"To love Him and love others."

"Was what you just said and did to your brother loving him like God made you to do?"

"No."

"Then you are not fulfilling the purpose for which God created you. You need to pray and ask the Lord to forgive you. You need to ask your brother to forgive you. How should you have responded to your brother?"

These conversations are consistently bringing the child back to truth and reminding them of their relationship with God as the motivation and power to live godly and be all that they were created to be.

A child's first lessons in life are simple ones that reap a multitude of blessings. The child simply must be taught to respect and obey their parents (or those in authority over them). This is developed through diligent, consistent, loving instruction & discipline. The parent must be careful to seek to win their child's heart. Not by spoiling them and giving them what they want all the time, but by proving yourself to be someone who is for them. This is done by being trustworthy to provide consistent, diligent, trustworthy loving discipline and direction. The child must see and believe that you are for them, truly! Not merely giving them their way and not disciplining them because you are angry, but doing things for their good. You must speak truth constantly to them. When they are acting or speaking in a manner contrary to godliness you should simply speak truth by directing their words & actions. Lastly, take advantage of opportunities to be on their side. Be for them, especially in the presence of other people. Do things they want to do. Remember, you may know the outcome beforehand but they are still living experimentally. Experiment with them for their sake.

Teen Years

Teen years goal:
Assisting them to walk out their true identity as they traverse this land. Continuing to build on their firm foundation in Christ by building deeper intimacy of the knowledge of who God is. Teaching them to trust Him in all things.

As we continue in the training of our children we will hit a bump in the road, for some a little bump, for others it is major. The child who, for the most part, received information willingly and openly, all of a sudden (more gradual for others), starts questioning the input he has been given. He is now asking "why."

Many parents misinterpret this as rebellion or disrespect when their child is simply transitioning to another stage in life. They are growing and maturing as the Lord has created them to do, and are no longer satisfied in just being given the facts. They want to understand WHY it is so. This is when you go deeper in explaining to your child about their God and His ways.

In our home we don't usually hit major bumps in the road at this point. We believe it's due to the fact that within the information we are giving our children during the rote memory stage lies the answers to their "Why's." So when they start questioning within themselves "Why is this so?" the answer pops up in their spirit before the question is completely formed. They have been given the tools to work with. They begin to use them without needing much guidance.

Of course there are those children that are a bit more strong willed or logic based who will require quite a bit more hands on discipleship. It is important that we don't forget to require respect and honor of parents and those in authority in this stage. Don't be afraid or intimidated by the "Why" questions. Be honest and open with your children. You don't have to have all the answers on hand. But you need to let them know you know the One who has all the answers. Explore and journey together as you seek out the answer to the question you may not be able to answer. But do explore, do seek it out. This process is very important for building a strong foundation and a strong relationship with your child.

Make your answers Bible based.

As you respond to your children's inquiries, resist the temptation to answer out of your experience, reason, logic or wisdom alone, doing so ultimately says to a child, "Do whatever you feel or think is right", instead respond to your child from the wisdom that God gives through His word. If you don't know God's wisdom on a topic, search your topic at *DesiringGod.org* and use this as a resource to study and learn God's perspective. Have your child join you in this journey because the goal is not the answer to the question but the process of the journey. You want your child to learn to and enjoy seeking God and studying His word for His ways. Remember, the goal is not the answer. This time of searching may bring revelations about unrelated topics that serve to mold the heart to maturity in Christ. Let the Spirit lead you.

Trust Jesus in this process. He is parenting your child through the work he is doing in you. The maturing of your child will be accomplished through the maturing and growth of you, the parent. Grow in Jesus. Let Him form you and grow you daily. Pursue Him in daily, quiet, one on one time.

Questions to Ponder

1) What is the greatest challenge this chapter has presented to your parenting?

2) What parenting goals do you have?

3) What is one of the goals for the primary years?

4) Consider a situation where utilizing these simple truth catechisms would have been beneficial in dealing with your child.

5) What is the goal for a child who is more logic based?

Chapter 5
Walk the Walk and Talk the Talk

You have to live the way you want your children to live. If you live one way and tell your child to live another, don't expect success in your parenting. If you teach them not to lie, you must not lie. Not even in joking or games. If you tell them they need to go to church, you must live out the need to go to church in your life. It is a powerful witness in the life of a child when your words and actions are the same. You cannot live differently than how you expect them to live. Typically your children will not live in a way that is contradictory to your example.

When we were young, one of the popular parental sayings was, "Do as I say and not as I do." It excused parents to do things that they considered inappropriate and wrong for their children to do while allowing them to place expectations upon their children that they did not uphold in their lives. I hope this sounds like utter nonsense to you, because it is.

Children learn by what is modeled to them just as much as by what they are told. This means you must be the person you are training your children to become. You will see your worst traits in your children. So if you plan to have children, start by training yourself. They will replicate your actions.

If you want your children to be honest, don't justify it when you lie. If you want your children to be respectful, you need to respect others as a normal practice in your life. Don't think that you can "act good" when your children are watching and not let them see your bad behavior. Your children will even copy your secret sinful actions. It is as if your behavior is visited upon your children genetically, it isn't, but it seems that way.

This is Where You Begin

This means that the first act of training children is to train your own behavior. Make an honest assessment of your behavior and identify the areas that need to be erased. Identify the traits that you do not want reproduced in your children and diligently work to remove them from your life. This especially applies to sins, your secret sins or habitual sins or regular sins will open the door for your children to be brought up in the same mold. They may not take on your family destroying addiction to alcohol, but it may reproduce itself as an addiction to food or TV or some other potentially vile trait. You must work on you. Then, as a parent, you just have to be yourself.

Walk the walk and talk the talk. Be the person that you want your children to become. This does not mean that you must have perfect actions all the time; if we could do that, the death and resurrection of Jesus for our sins would have been unnecessary, all we would need is the will to be good and, Shazam! we would be saved by will power. No, perfection lies in the pursuit of righteousness even in our failures. There will be times when you have to repent to your children and ask forgiveness, but isn't that what you want them to do? That is walking the walk.

Walk the Walk and Talk the Talk

Do some serious, steal away, time alone, prayerful, meditative soul searching. Make an honest assessment of yourself. See your sins and weaknesses the way God sees them.

Temper?

Lie on tax returns?

Lie on the phone? "Tell them I am not here"

Lie on social media?

Addictive behavior? "I can say no but I don't choose to"

Gossip?

Lust?

Procrastinator?

Irresponsible?

Manipulator?

Abusive?

Secrets?

Lazy, slothful?

Immature?

People pleaser?

Materialistic?

Anorexic?

Glutton?

Neglectful?

Uncaring?

Self destructive?

Jealous?

Pride?

Slander?

Self centered? Selfish?

Always have an excuse, never a repentant heart?

Violent?

Foul mouth?

Deceitful?

Spineless?

Fake?

Untrustworthy?

Don't keep your word?

This list keeps going. Take a long look in the mirror then pray and ask God to remove these things from your character and replace them with righteous traits that you would be proud for your children to imitate. Traits that reflect the Christ in you. Then begin the process of the replacement. To do this, study the Bible to see what it says about putting off your traits and putting on holy ones in their place. Learn God's ways and become transformed by the renewal of your mind. This is a change that is not merely external but internal in nature, and it is the internal nature that your children will pick up on. They will read you like a book, so invite them like Paul invited us in the Bible, "Follow me as I follow Christ."

Ephesians 5:10 says,

Find out what pleases the Lord.

Make this your life pursuit and remember, God gives the power to change. Hallelujah! So we pursue change by making purposeful steps to pursue Him. This is somewhat counterintuitive. Intuition would say, pursue change by making purposeful steps to change, but this indirect method is actually the direct way to change. The closer you get to God, the more you become what He wants you to be.

Is there a discipline that you can add to your schedule that will bring about deeper intimacy with God?

How to Not be a Hypocrite

There may possibly be some battles that are not won overnight. Battles between the old man and the new man in you. Secret sins or habitual sins may have such a strong hold by the time you reach parenthood that they require a fight that must be persistent. To this I say fight and fight to the death. Never give up, trust the God that lives in you to overcome.

How do you train your children to walk in victory in areas you have been or are defeated? How do you require them to say 'no' where you have said 'yes' far too often? How do you not be a hypocrite when you train them unto righteousness while you struggle with unrighteousness?

I hope that this is never your struggle or circumstance. But I am sure it will be for some. The answer is to bring your struggle into the light, let others in to know how your flesh or the devil pulls you to stray from righteousness and enlist their help, be humble and repentant of heart, confess your sins and let God cleanse you of unrighteousness, then go and sin no more. Do this by not giving opportunity to your weakness and pursuing God's help vehemently. Your children need to learn how to pursue righteousness in the midst of their own failure, they need to know how to repent and how to be humble, how to not always give excuses for their failure, how to be broken because they broke the heart of God and not just because they were caught, how to "tell on" themselves and not wait to be caught, how to want righteousness and not allow the satisfaction or lure of unrighteousness to deceive them. Tell your children of your struggles to whatever degree is appropriate and have them pray with and for you. They are already watching you and see and know more than you would like them to. Let them join in appropriately keeping you accountable (we say appropriately because you are still the adult. You are still their parent and they still have to respect you.) The battle is to be won at all costs. Not winning the battle is to give the enemy a stronghold that may pass on generationally. Don't give your struggles to your children. Give them the resolve to overcome at any cost. Remember, will power is not the source of your victory, but faith, love and obedience. Increase your faith in and love for God. Work on this relationship as it is your freedom.

Questions to Ponder

1) What is the first act of training children?

2) Does your character reflect what you want your child's character to be?

3) What traits are present in your life that you do not want replicated in your children?

4) How do you train your children to walk in victory in areas you have been or are defeated?

Chapter 6
Authority

Parental authority is how you move when you believe that parents and children are not equals when it comes to decision making and areas of discipline. Parents and children are equal in some things, like being recipients of the saving grace of God. Parents are not saved differently than children. But in other things, the roles of parent and child are not the same. We should not treat our children as if they have equal input or overriding authority when they do not. In areas of decision making and discipline, parents have a greater responsibility from God, more maturity, more experience, and more knowledge. They are to use these things to train up their children. You should not give your child equal input in these areas, there is far too much for them to learn before they gain the wisdom to make wise choices. Not to mention, there is far too much "self" that must be crucified before they learn to think and move unselfishly. This is not to say that you, as a parent, are the picture of perfection,

Authority

but God expects children to honor and obey their parents in a way that shows respect for their parent's authority.

I watched a parent with her 6 year old daughter trying to get her daughter to stop what she was doing and do what the parent wanted the child to do. The mom reasoned with the child to try to get her to agree to the priority of her request. She tried to get the child to agree to stopping her present activity and agree to the logic of the mom and agree to do what was being asked. Parents that don't know and exercise their authority tend to be permissive. They can't tell the child no or correct them, and tend to treat the child like an equal. It is almost as if they are intimidated by their children. They are hesitant to tell them to do anything. There is no one in charge.

To the thoughtful child, attempting to reason, rather than giving clear directions, causes the child to move as if the weight of the world is on his or her shoulders. The child becomes bound instead of free to enjoy their childhood within the confines of a safe and secure structure. Please don't expect your child to take a role in parenting themselves. You be the parent and let the child be the child. There will be a time for them to learn and mimic your parenting ability. That time is not during their childhood.

Some Actions That Speak Loudly of the Lack of Authority

Continual threats reflect lack of authority. Not following through with consequences to bad behavior reflects lack of authority. Ignoring or not noticing defiant behavior reflects lack of authority. Not disciplining rude or disrespectful behavior is a sign of lack of authority. Allowing the escalation of your emotions before you act, acting out of escalated emotion, arguing, these show no authority. No pre-consideration of actions and consequences, no pre-discussed identification of acceptable and unacceptable actions, these are displays of no authority. Fear, as opposed to anticipating response to anticipated bad behavior, is a sign of no authority.

Authority looks like confidence. It gives off the fragrance of "in control" and "under control." It speaks of pre-established consequences and is followed by follow through. It does not wait to be justified in the eyes of others. It acts on instinct. It quickly responds to openly defiant rebellion. It does not always assume the worst but neither does it always assume the best. It is humble, quick to repent, and apologizes publicly when an alleged infraction was identified publicly. When it is being exercised, it is not open to interpretation, cross examination, approval of the majority, judgement or argument. It is not a response to pent up emotion.

Love Saturated Authority

To paint the complete picture we must talk about love saturated authority. Authority is not merely heavy handed discipline. It is the consideration of what is best for a child and creating the environment that will allow that child to take wings and fly. It is belief in your responsibility and ability to determine what is best for the growth of your child; and in most cases, it is making this determination independent of the child's input which is often skewed by immaturity, lack of experience, laziness, selfishness or self-centeredness. Your experience, maturity and priority of your child allow you to consider a much broader array of information. At the very least, it gives you the basis to pursue and learn what is needed to make wise decisions regarding your child's maturation.

God says in Hebrews that He only disciplines those He loves as his own children and it brings about the peaceable fruit of righteousness. Love saturated authority involves discipline exercised for the fruit of righteousness in a child. That means discipline for the sake of heart transformation, not just for the sake of quiet or cleanliness, or out of anger and frustration. Authority saturated in love is authority that is for the child. Children sense this and will draw near as they feel their needs are your concern. It brings peace to their heart. It provides walls and restrictions that bring order so that they don't have to feel as if they are flailing. If you ever move a newborn too quickly, you will see their little arms instinctively fly out from their sides and their mouths fly open in fear and their bodies tense. This feeling of insecurity is a shock to the system and destroys peace. Newborns prefer being swaddled tightly and held close, near familiar sounds and smells. We never lose the need for a protective surrounding that causes the soul to be bathed in peace. Loving authority involves limiting a child's world for the child's good.

Developing Unchallenged Respect for Your Authority

When you establish authority in your little ones it must be unquestioned. There are some actions and attitudes that you must not allow. Please don't allow your child to question your authority. No asking, "Why?" at an early elementary age. "Why" is not a declaration of curiosity and question in the attempt to gain knowledge. No, "Why" at this stage is a tool in an attempt to get one's own way. Your child will not ask why you let them do what they want to do, "Why" is only for those things that the child does not want.

Please acknowledge this and establish a "No Why" policy. In its place teach your child a "Yes mommy", "Yes daddy" policy. Your child's reasoning abilities will develop later and there will be a time for you to explain your actions as part of the process of teaching your child to be an adult, but that time is not in early childhood.

Please don't allow your child to respond to your instruction with an explanation of what they are doing or why they are doing it.

Parent: "Turn the video games off now, your time is over."
Child: "I still have 5 minutes because I went to the bathroom."

Your authority is not a court of law and your child is not a lawyer trying to win their case. This would mean that the winner is the one who can best argue their case. This is defiant of the fact that God has established parental authority over children and instructed children to obey and honor it. Teach your children to respond with a title of respect; "Yes mommy", "Yes daddy"; and present their request as a question.

Parent: "Turn the video games off now, your time is over."
Child: "Yes mommy. I went to the bathroom, may I play for 5 more minutes?"

This acknowledges and respects authority and that pleases God. We want our children to be pleasing to God.

Please God

That is the goal, to teach our children to know and love God so that their hearts desire is to please Him. We are not trying to train little robots that impress strangers through their obedience to their parents. We are not after an outward display. We are after the heart. A heart that knows its creator and its purpose in creation. A heart that lives in intimate relationship with its creator.

Which do I Teach First, Love or Obedience?

Teach love. As a parent you must know that obedience is an act of love and you must teach your children this. You must realize that not teaching obedience means you are not loving your child as you should. We have managed somehow to separate love and obedience, they are different but not separable. Jesus said, if you love me you will keep my commandments. Hebrews says the Lord disciplines the one he loves. Psalms says, a father disciplines the son he delights in. Do not separate discipline and love. Do not make discipline a consequence of anger or disappointment. See your training in obedience as the pruning of a rose bush. I don't cut away branches of the rose bush because I want to punish it, I cut them for its good, so that it will blossom to the fullness of its ever increasing potential.

Questions to Ponder

1) What actions speak loudly of the lack of authority?

2) What does authority look like?

3) How does authority move?

4) What is authority saturated in love?

Chapter 7
Puberty and the Teenage Years

Whether it's from our own personal experience of going through the "teen years", or from raising teenage children, we all know the adolescent years can be turbulent and disrupting to everything we knew prior. But what we don't tend to talk about is how exciting these turbulent years can be when we gain the correct perspective of what is truly happening within our young people in this season of life. When the adults gain perspective, they can then help their young people gain a proper outlook and help them journey through this rocky period with a little more grace and better balance.

Parenting for the teen years actually begins much earlier as you develop your family as a wonderful place to be. As you love being with your children, family becomes a fun place, a loving place, a desired place, a safe place. Of course, you must want to be with your children when they are younger. Don't look at your children as if they are a bother or hindrance to your life. You are not punishing them or holding them back by requiring them to spend time with you rather than going away to be with friends. Family is important. The appreciation and expectation of togetherness is so extremely important during the teen years that you should not wait until the teen years to build it. Enjoy spending time together and do it purposely. Don't develop a habit where your children find their fun, entertainment, or relax time always away from you, or doing things without you. This especially applies to your children hiding away in their room or on electronic devices. Alone time for your children is important and should be nurtured, but you must also nurture a healthy balance of family togetherness.

Togetherness is Vital

Walking through puberty with a child can test you. And that test could last for 4 or 5 years. This is such a huge topic that it deserves a lot of respect so I will discuss it in parts. These parts will together develop the perspectives that will get you through a tough time of puberty with a child.

First, know that this stage is not the same for any two children. Children will act and react differently to what is going on inside them during this stage. It is for this reason that there is no "one size fits all" way to walk through puberty with your child. We have had the privilege of observing 6 of our children navigate this stage of life. Each child responded differently, struggled differently and matured differently.

Define Puberty from God's Perspective

We often talk about the concept that was made popular by Henry Blackaby, "look to see where God is at work and join him there." (Blackaby, 2007) Many people have difficulty figuring out what God is doing at any given time in their life. Well, puberty is possibly the easiest time of life to know for sure what God is doing. It is at this time that He is doing the same thing in all people. It is during this time that God transforms children into adults. On purpose and by design, God uses this stage of life to transform a child mentally, emotionally and physically into adulthood. A child goes from childhood to being capable of having children and being a parent. It is an obvious physical process in which the body changes in many ways. More importantly it is a mental process that changes outlooks and perspectives toward self, others and responsibility. It is such an important time of life that we should never leave it to itself. This should be a time of very active parenting.

So What Happens During Puberty

In our family we take our children out to dinner, desert and a talk with mommy and daddy. We inadvertently began a tradition of going to Sammy's Wood Fired Pizza and allowing our children to order the Messy Sundae with their meal. Our puberty talk has become known as the Messy Sundae talk. We once transcribed this talk for our children to use with their children. The following is a transcript of one of those Messy Sundae talks.

Tatiana, if you were to think about all the things that Jesus did while he was on earth, there would be a lot. But if you were to name something that Jesus was capable of doing by himself while he was on earth, Jesus would interrupt the conversation and He would say what He said in John 5:19, read it to me.

> *"Very truly I tell you, the Son can do nothing by himself; he can do only what he sees his Father doing, because whatever the Father does the Son also does."*

Jesus watched what the father was doing and joined Him in it. "Whatever the Father does, the Son also does." And we do the same thing. We look to see what God is doing and we join him there. Seeing what God is doing is never easier than watching what he is doing right now in your life. You see, right now, God is at work changing you. He is taking you through a process that will ultimately change you from being a child to being an adult that is able to have children and handle the responsibilities of being a parent.

It is a beautiful process that can take 4 to 5 years before He is done. And the way He does it is different for every person. In some people He begins this process at 9 or 10 years old . In others it may not start until 12 or 13. You have no say in when it starts. God puts that information into the DNA of every person and it goes according to His design and desire. And the beauty of this is that He has taken every person on the planet and every person that has ever been on the planet, through this process and stage of life. This is a God thing and it is what God is doing and we praise Him for it.

The Pituitary

So what happens is that at a certain pre-arranged time, your body activates a little gland that is located right there in your neck. It is called the pituitary gland and it becomes the command center for everything that will take place. It produces the little engines that will run around in your body sparking all types of changes. These engines are called hormones and the pituitary produces them and sends them out to do their work to grow and change your body and mind. The goal of this process is to make you into an adult that is actively taking on responsibility for yourself and others, capable of having children and capable of deep thoughts about an intimate relationship with God.

Physically

As we walk through this time together you will begin to see God at work in your body bringing about lots of changes. Physically you may get taller or you may get heavier so we will watch your diet and exercise. Your face may break out with acne, we will be attentive to your skin care also. Your body may start having body odor after physical activity. You will probably be a lot more tired and sleep more because your body will need your energy to accomplish these changes. You will begin to grow body hair. Some people have a lot and some have a little but you will begin to grow hair probably on your legs, under your arms and between your legs. Your breasts will grow sometime during this process. This is part of the preparation for parenthood.

Puberty and the Teenage Years

God intends for you to be able to nurture a child to life one day.

The things that will take place within you to transform you for parenthood are complex and beautiful. God has designed you to be able to bring forth and carry a new life. During puberty He begins to get your body ready for that purpose. During puberty your body will start producing eggs. These eggs are not like chicken eggs but they can become a new life if the conditions are right. Your body will produce one egg each month from your ovaries which are located below your stomach. You have two ovaries, one on the right and one on the left, so they alternate each month producing an egg and that egg goes into your uterus. This process will happen every month from the day it starts until the day it stops which is usually when you are near 50 years old. Most women can no longer have children after the age of 50 because their body does not produce eggs any more. This is why it was so amazing that Abraham's wife had a child when she was nearly 100 years old. That was a huge miracle.

You will produce an egg each month but it will only become a new life if it is connected with a sperm and you don't produce sperm. Sperm is produced in men. That egg will sit in your uterus and die in a matter of days. That dead egg would infect your body and make you sick, but God has a beautiful design. It works like this, your body sends blood to your uterus. If that egg becomes a new life, the blood carries the nutrients to the egg so that it can grow. But if the egg dies, the blood washes the egg out of the body through your vagina and cleans you so that you do not become infected and sick. This happens every month at the same time of the month. It is called a period or cycle.

Why This Cycle?

The blood brings life and washes away death. There is power in the blood. What blood do you know of that brings life and washes us white as snow? Yes, the blood of Jesus. The beauty of your period is that God reminds you every month of the sacrifice of His son Jesus to give you new life and wash away your sins completely. It serves as something to remember

Jesus by and reminds you of God's great love so you can walk as a new child of God.

Each month your period will come and your body will go through the cycle of blood cleansing your uterus and passing out your vagina. Your mother will help prepare you because we don't know exactly when it will start. In some girls their cycle is painful, but the pain must never override the beauty of this representation. We are saved by the blood.

The Changes in the Mind

Through puberty your body will see all these physical changes but it will also see emotional and mental changes. Here we have to be careful because all the work that the hormones are doing in your body can serve to overwhelm your mind and thoughts. Some girls go through puberty and struggle with doing right relationships and doing relationships right. Sometimes their best friend today will be their hated enemy tomorrow and their best friend again next week. Hopefully your mind will not ride that roller coaster but if it does we will help you to navigate your emotions so that you do not move in your relationships like that. Some girls will go through the need for approval. They will want to be accepted by their girl friends and want the attention of boys. This is out of balance if you find yourself changing who you are or what you look like for the approval of other children. We will help you walk through these emotions and will put in place limitations that will keep you from the pressure of conformity. We will support your mind with truth so that you combat lies about who you are and whose you are. You are a child of the most high King and He loves you with a purpose for how he has designed you and positioned you. With your mind doing so much growing and changing, this is not the time to enter into relationships with boys.

The Boy Talk

Speaking of boys, each of your brothers had a talk with us also. Their talk time started the same because they too need to know the importance of watching God and joining Him in what He is doing. They need to know that God is active in their lives and they need to know what He is doing during this stage in life. But the rest of the talk is different because their bodies are different and their minds are different. Their talk proceeds like this:

If you were to think about all the things that Jesus did while he was on earth, there would be a lot. But if you were to name something that Jesus was capable of doing by himself while he was on earth, Jesus would interrupt the conversation and He would say what He said in John 5:19, read it to me.

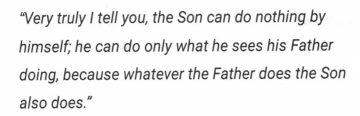

"Very truly I tell you, the Son can do nothing by himself; he can do only what he sees his Father doing, because whatever the Father does the Son also does."

See actually, Jesus watched what His father was doing and joined Him in it. "Whatever the Father does, the Son also does." And we do the same thing. We look to see what God is doing and we join him there. Seeing what God is doing is never easier than watching what he is doing right now in your life. You see, right now, God is at work changing you. He is completely changing you from being a child to being a young man. There is a difference and I could sum up the difference like this: A young man has grown in responsibility for others; A young man has learned how to love a woman; and a young man is able to have a child and establish a heritage by teaching that child to know and love God, Jesus and the Holy Spirit.

Responsibility

So during this time, God is going to grow you in responsibility. This means that you will be taking on more decision making tasks and learning to move in consideration of others.

Here is what I mean;
When you were a newborn child you would get hungry every 3 hours and sometimes you would announce to the world that you were hungry by crying. By crying you were saying, "I want what I want

and I want it now." You were completely selfish in your consideration. You never considered the needs of your mother as a newborn child, "Mom I'm hungry but I see you're really tired and you have not gotten any rest so why don't you get a little rest first." No, you were just hungry and you would cry louder and louder until you got what you wanted. And that is normal for a child; but for that child to become a young man he must grow in responsibility to others. He must learn to see the needs of others, even when considering his own needs, and respond in consideration of the needs of others. "Mom, I'm hungry, would you like me to fix lunch today?" "Mom, it's lunch time and we are out of bread, would you like me to run to the store and get some?"

So during this time of your life God will be changing you from a self centered child to a young man that considers the needs of others. He will be giving you situations so you can learn to see and consider the needs of others. So look out for times that will seem to be and feel unfair. Things like having someone mistreat you and you respond in anger then you get in trouble for it. God is developing in you a greater sense of responsibility. He is not trying to develop in you a sense of justice and fairness right now. He is working to get you to see the hurts and needs of others and to respond to that. This is the kind of responsibility that a man must show for others and puberty is when you learn it.

Why do You Need to Learn Responsibility for Others?

The purpose of God changing a child to an adult is always with a view to family. If not your own family someday then God's family, the church. In God's family everyone plays a part and has a grace given role that contributes to the building up of the family. As a young man you must grow in responsibility for others so that you can be responsible for the tender care of a wife someday, and/or the God fearing training of a child, and/or the building up of the church. Whichever call God may place on your life, you must grow out of the selfishness of childhood and *into manhood where you take on responsibility for others.*

As your parents we will join with God in what he is doing and walk with you through this time. Your level of expected responsibility will increase. Things like your bedtime will change, your chores will change, you will see freedoms that allow you space to practice making wise decisions and we will talk through your decision making to learn the difference between a wise decision and a selfish decision.

You Must Learn to Love a Woman

This second point is so important. The example of how to do this is none less than Jesus Himself and how he loves his bride. The bride of Christ is the church and a man is to love his wife as Christ loves the church. That's what the Bible says in Ephesians 5.

> *"Husbands, love your wives, as Christ loved the church."*

To learn to love a woman, God has graciously given us mothers (and sisters). We learn to love a woman by loving our mother. We must grow to love our mother with a, "you're more important than me, sacrifice what I want, serve you" kind of love. It's a "talking, communicating, share your heart" kind of love. It's a "cherishing, listening, want to be with you" kind of love.

It is NOT a "romantic, attracted to you" kind of love. That rides on the wings of emotion. This is a " commitment, committed for life" kind of love that finds roots regardless of the other person's flaws. This love grows by taking responsibility for the care, provision and protection of another and showing them honor.

In puberty God is growing you to learn to love a woman, not growing you to love "women". This lesson is not learned by dating or having girlfriends during puberty. The values found in dating/girlfriend experiences are not the values that God is teaching you through puberty. Girlfriend relationships actually serve to hinder the things that God is working in you as He takes you out of childhood and into manhood. As the impact of hormones in your body increases, you will have the desire to experience exclusive intimate relationships with girls but we will stay the course of joining the work that God is doing. We will not yield to desires of the flesh. We will encourage you elsewhere and we will not go there. There is a time for these relationships but it is not during your training through puberty into manhood.

Changes in the Body

So far I have told you about the things that God will be doing in your heart and mind as you go through the next several years. But He has also designed for you to go through physical changes in your body as you go through this stage. Your body will change from a child's body to a man's body.

You will experience lots of changes. You will grow rapidly and get taller. Your feet will grow a lot. You get hair on your body, under your arms, around your penis, maybe facial hair and chest hair. You will start to get body odor when you sweat. You voice will change and you will notice your voice cracking when you talk,

Then there will be lots of changes that will happen with your penis besides growing hair. Up to now your penis is just used for where your urine comes out, but God designed your penis for more than that. This is where your sperm will come out. Sperm is what carries your DNA and when it joins an egg in a woman it passes that information to a baby. Up to now your body does not make sperm because a child's body does not make sperm. But during puberty your body will tell itself to start making sperm. Sperm is made in your testicles and it is creamy white when it comes out of your penis not liquidy yellow like urine. When your body starts making sperm you will know because it will come out of your penis. This usually happens at night while you are sleeping and you will think you have wet your pants. It is called a wet dream. Don't worry, this is part of the process that God is doing to grow you as a young man. When that happens, when you have a wet dream, let me know.

Another thing that will happen to your penis is that at times it will get really hard and straight. This is because it is filling up with blood and that will make it firm and perk up. This can be embarrassing because sometimes it just happens and you can't stop it or make it go away. It goes away on its own in a few minutes but in the meantime you have an embarrassing bump in your pants. This is part of this process also.

Stages

God is making your body ready to be a parent and have children. This process is not just physical but also mental. Your mind will go through growing changes during this time as well. The changes in your mind can be deceiving and overwhelming. Everyone experiences this period differently.

You could go through the "I don't want" stage. This is when you want to stop doing all the things you loved doing as a child. Or you may doubt the upbringing of your parents and want to live a different way. Here again we will help you stay the course. With your mind going through so many changes, this is not a good time to change from the things that we saw God developing in you as a child. And it is not the time to venture away from the teaching and practices that we have developed in you from early on for God's glory and your good. We will help you keep steady and navigate this process so that you come out of it with clarity of purpose.

You could go through the "Nobody understands me" stage. This is when your mind plays tricks on you and tells you that the people that have loved you the longest now love you the least and the people that have known you the least now love you the most. During this time you could doubt the love of your parents, the ones who cleaned you when you pooped on yourself, cleaned up after your vomit, provided all your clothing, food and transportation, and happily adjusted their lives to care for you. You could begin to think that those that have loved you the longest now don't understand you and love you the least. Then you may begin thinking that your friends, other children that have known you the least, now are the ones that "get you" and love you the most. We will remind you everyday that no one loves you or has loved you as much as we do and have loved you. When your mind tells you that our actions as parents (that feel to you like unfair restrictions in the moment) are not loving, we will remind you of our love and the track record of our love. We love you now and will forever like no other.

There is also the "What happened to my loving little boy" stage. This is where you forget all the ways of being loving that you learned as a child and become harsh and rude. We will remind you of the loving ways of God and keep you considering others in your interactions and communications.

You could go through the grunt stage. This is where your mind wants to stop formulating sentences and complete thoughts and you want to respond to questions with single words and sounds. It is very important that you begin learning to communicate your thoughts and ideas so we will often hold conversations with you where you must share your feelings and thoughts about how something impacts you.

Why is My Mind Going Through These Stages?

Ultimately you are learning to pass on a heritage and teach another person, like your child, to know and love God. This is called parenting. God is not just readying you to have children physically but he is preparing you mentally to have children and that means to parent them so that they know and love God.

The End

Marriage Effects on Puberty

We know that puberty can be a tough time for our young people to get a grip on their emotions, perspectives and priorities. But, the difficulty is magnified significantly if your marriage relationship is broken or breaking. Sometimes single parenthood is the hand that God has dealt us in life. But you must know that the work that you put into your marriage to keep it healthy, affects everyone around you.

A mother came to us to get help with her son who was subtly rebelling and in the early stages of puberty. He was not wildly rebellious but it was clear that he was being purposely defiant to his parents. As we spoke to this mom who was convinced that her son's actions were the result of puberty and wanted to know what to do about it, we came to questions about her marriage. The mother was immediately quiet and then tearful. Their marriage was struggling. Their son, who was already struggling in the throes of puberty, was now feeling the totally unsettling insecurity of a life that was out of control and he had no idea of what to do.

Purposeful Parenting

Your marriage struggles will affect your children at every stage of their development. During puberty this effect is compounded. So what do you do? We all have marriage struggles sometimes. The answer is communication. Communication between parents and children. Communication between mom and dad. Communication will help our children learn to weather the storms that they will one day experience. Learn, practice, do and teach communication in your family.

Puberty and the Teenage Years

Chapter 8
Results

Here is where I give you the guarantee that if you follow the precepts outlined in this book your children will turn out perfect every time. Only there is no guarantee. At least not here. There are guarantees in life, thank God. God is faithful, guaranteed. You are a big sinner raising little sinners and all of you would remain as such if it were not for the sacrifice of Jesus Christ, guaranteed. But to say your children will turn out perfect, no guarantee.

I had the privilege of walking with a dear friend as he contemplated the recent death of his father. It was a very hard and sad time made worse because my friend had no reason to believe that his dad had received Jesus as his savior and the promise of eternity with God. As he shared he said, "My father rejected salvation many times. He heard and knew God's plan of salvation and chose each time to have nothing to do with God. I believe that a gracious God will not withhold from my dad his desire and choice. I believe my dad is in hell right now."

There is a stinging discomfort in the harshness of that reality. Though we know it to be true of every person that does not receive God's plan of salvation, saying it out loud feels disrespectful or wrong somehow. Your children must make the choice to follow Jesus. All your parental training, discipleship, love and leading will ensure that they know truth as they make that decision and it makes it easier for them to side with truth, but it will not make it impossible for them to choose to not follow God.

So we parent with the wisdom of the thoughts laid out in this book not because it will guarantee perfect results, but because parenting with Godly wisdom is our act of obedience performed to find and know the pleasure of God. Our statement of faith is, "Results belong to God." Trust Him with your children.

Questions to Ponder

1) As parents, what is our act of obedience?

Results

Chapter 9
You do You Boo Boo

Building a Culture in Your Family

Part of parenting is establishing a culture in your home. How do we communicate? How do we interact? How do we deal with sin? What are the calendar non-negotiables? How do we value others? How do we make major decisions? What is the importance of togetherness? How do we celebrate each other? What traditions do we have and why? What are we purposely growing our hearts and minds towards and how do we do it? What are our family priorities?

How do we define good family culture?

 Culture: *The set of shared attitudes, values, goals, and practices that characterizes an institution or organization.*

Culture is the fertilizer that feeds the growth of what we want to produce.

A story about values:

Kenyan runner Abel Mutai was only a few meters from the finish line at the Olympics, but got confused with the signs and stopped, thinking he had finished the race. A Spanish man, Ivan Fernandez, was right behind him and, realizing what was going on, started shouting to the Kenyan to keep running. Mutai did not know Spanish and did not understand.

Realizing what was going on, Fernandez pushed Mutai to victory.

A reporter asked Ivan, "Why did you do this?" Ivan replied, "My dream is that one day we can have some sort of community life where we push ourselves and also others to win."

> *The reporter insisted "But why did you let the Kenyan win?" Ivan replied, "I didn't let him win, he was going to win. The race was his."*
>
> *The reporter insisted and asked again, "But you could have won!" Ivan looked at him and replied: "But what would be the merit of my victory? What would be the honor of this medal? What would my Mother think of it?"*
>
> *Values are transmitted from generation to generation. What values do we teach our children and how much do you inspire others to win? Most of us take advantage of people's weaknesses instead of helping to strengthen them.*

Culture is the official and unofficial traditions of your family. It will form the basis of how your family is defined, and it will do this whether you think through this step of purposely defining culture or not. If you go on vacation every year, it will foster the anticipation of going away, being together and making memories. Do you celebrate birthdays? It will establish the mindset that one day a year the fact that I am special will be celebrated and I will receive gifts to that end. Family game nights develop confidence in being together as a family and love for each other. Date night develops confidence in the marriage bond and security in the structure and design of the family. Praying and/or reading before bedtime develops security and safety in the minds of young children and the enjoyment of these actions as a pastime. Everything that you do regularly has a cultural impact on your family. Take the time to think about what kind of cultural impact you want to establish and what regular actions you will do to support that culture.

Family culture tends to be a combination of the input from both parents. It is a continuation of the traditions that had the strongest positive impression on you as a child, and your reaction to the things that you most disliked in your childhood. It is beneficial to talk through these things so that the culture you develop is purposefully positive and not just a knee jerk reaction to your upbringing.

Families are God's design. He made them on purpose and for a purpose. Families are God's way of passing on to the next generation who God is and what he has done. In our family we do this through family devotions and spending time in the word, or as we put it, "Gathering around the things of God." This could be prayer, worship, scripture reading or bible study, all of these establish culture that honors God.

Developing a culture within your family will bring a sense of belonging, this sense of belonging will promote a feeling of security which in turn will foster confidence and loyalty in your children as they perceive that they are part of something bigger than themselves.

The concept of belonging is not only utilized by those who want to produce great results in their children. Actually, the idea of belonging is something effectively utilized by gangs. The culture within inner city gangs develops such a strong sense of belonging that they become a family of their own. The culture you create in your family will establish the beauty of togetherness, or lack thereof, along with every other attribute of your family.

A Story About Culture

Many parents complain that their teenagers don't want to be with them. They say this is typical. It is not typical, it is trained. It is the fruit of the culture that you have established in your home. Typical is what you allow in your home, and allow in your relationships. It has not been my experience as a parent or as a teenager that teenagers don't want to be with their parents. As a teenager I enjoyed the presence of my parents, our relationship was rich and I wanted to be with them. As a mother of 7 children (two of which are 16 & 18 as I am writing this) I am finding that my teenagers want me to be around, and always include me in their late night movie nights. They have their friends, but they enjoy their parents.

It is important that I state here that as parents, we never made it our goal to become our children's friends. They don't need more friends but they do need parents. They need responsible adults who can lovingly & graciously guide them in all truth. Someone who can make those difficult calls on their behalf. Someone willing to be the "bad guy" when necessary, but at the same time willing to make sacrifices for the sake of the child just to encourage them in their gifting. Sometimes sacrifice looks like taking her and her friends to the midnight showing of that new movie being released. Other times it will be the two of you planning, baking for and executing a tea just for the two of you.

Think back to when your teenagers were young, did you want to be with your children when they were growing up, or was it usually your desire to be without your children? Did you enjoy them & voice your joy, or were you instead voicing your tiredness & frustration and left them feeling that they were the source of this? Who wants to be with people who don't, or in this case, didn't want to be with them?

In developing the culture of our family we plan date nights with our children. Even as young as 4 years old, they get alone time with mommy and/or daddy. This is a time to be together and hear what's on their hearts. It can get complicated trying to juggle date nights with 7 children or more, but they don't have to be every week or even every month. Establish a time frame that works for your family and enjoy them.

What I share with parents is not info based on extensive clinical experimentation or research. It is primarily based on experience, observation, principles gleaned from the word of God & good old fashioned revelation from the Spirit of God.

- Melissa

Questions to Ponder

1) What kind of cultural impact do you want to establish within your family?

2) What actions will you take to support your family culture?

3) What cultures can you establish in your family that honor God?

4) Do you express to your children your desire to, and joy in, being with them?

You do You Boo Boo

Chapter 10
The COVID Education Addendum

Thanks to COVID-19, we have all become homeschoolers to some degree. It is only fitting that we include at least a little addendum addressing that fact. What we want to give you here is a little understanding of how the brain develops and how this will impact learning, which will be helpful whether you are homeschooling or not.

There are 3 Primary Stages of Brain Development That are Associated With Classical Education.

Elementary Age, Grades K-5

Called the Grammar stage or Parrot stage.
This is where the nerves in the brain are forming connections. Children form habits and learn through memorization. They actually find memorization fun. They are sponges and absorb facts. Tell them stories,

teach them languages, teach them multiplication tables, teach them bible verses, teach them catechisms. Comprehension will come later. They are your little angels because, for the most part, they respond to you without question, argument or rebellion (if proper instruction, training & discipline have been applied). They absorb your words and actions or those of the people they spend the most time with. If they have a nanny that speaks another language they absorb the language. If they go to daycare they absorb the characteristics of their keepers and the other children.

This stage involves the learning of facts. Here we learn rules of spelling and phonics, rules of grammar, vocabulary of foreign languages, stories of history and literature, descriptions of plants, descriptions of animals, math facts like multiplication tables and more. This stage establishes the building blocks for use in the next stage.

Middle School, Grades 6-8

Called the Logic stage or Argumentative stage.

This is the "Why" stage. They question everything. All the lobes in the brain are working in overdrive here as the whole body steps up its activity to transform this little child into an adult, physically, mentally and spiritually. For the child, reasoning, motivation and morality are key players on the table and up for discussion. (Big side note here: If you taught them well in the Grammar stage, things like catechisms and memory verses, they will use that information to make logical connections here in the Logic stage.) Teach the elements of logical debate, sound premises and logical conclusions. In the Grammar stage you read to your child, in this stage, they read the book themselves and discuss with you the value and significance of the information and experiences in relation to the scope of their understanding of the world. They want to know why this is important to know and they want an answer they agree with. It must make logical sense in their forming minds (and that is not always going to happen). In this stage children want to know cause and effect. Logic puzzles and long conversations become tools of the trade.

This is the stage where logic is applied to all areas of study. In math we are no longer memorizing facts but learning the logic of algebra and algebraic manipulation. In writing we are learning paragraph construction and how to support a thesis. In reading we learn the criticism and analysis of texts, not just the absorption of information. In history a student must find out why the war of 1812 was fought rather than just reading its story. In science we learn the scientific method. Remember this is not a race where your child is smarter if they advance faster or do more rigorous work, the goal here is to mature your child into a teenager who argues logically, who thinks instead of reacts.

Just to make the toughest stage harder, allow me to add something here. This stage has the added treat of puberty to further complicate life. The contribution of the pituitary gland, and its host of hormones that direct the growth and maturity of the body at this stage means that there will be an unpredictable level of instability added to the equation. As much as this child wants to think logically here, they will at times act completely without any logic at all. The child that has played piano since 8 years old and is gifted, suddenly wants to stop playing. If you are the type of parent that wants your child to have many experiences and play several sports or play several instruments or act and be in the scouts, etc., then giving up something at this stage will not be a problem. But do not allow your child to give up their gifting or things that contribute to training them in their gifting. It is fine to put your foot down here.

When our oldest son was 16 years old and completely submerged in puberty, he came to us and told us he no longer wanted to play the violin because he was no good at it anyway. This was a shock to the system since Simeon had been happily playing the violin for 9 years at this point, and he was quite good. We spoke with him about his reasons and quickly deduced that there were other reasons for him coming to this conclusion, one of which was puberty (which he later named, The Fog). We listened to his concerns and desires. We also knew that he was gifted by God at playing the violin and it would possibly become a major part of his life. We told him that he would have to play the violin for one more year and give us all he had, at the end of the year we would talk again. Well today Simeon is a classically trained concert violinist with a Bachelors degree and Masters degree in Music Performance. The Fog will cloud your child's ability to make wise decisions; do not let it cloud your judgement in making wise decisions for your child, and do not let your child misdirect their future by agreeing with and accepting their misguided choices.

High School, Grades 9-12

The Rhetoric stage.

Here students learn the art of persuasive language. It is the communication and expression stage. Children learn to express what they understand in persuasive written and spoken words. All that they have learned in the previous two stages is put to use here to express original and convincing thoughts. This stage teaches students to think and articulate concepts. Subjects should incorporate research, writing and orating.

It is here that our children must develop a world view and understand right from wrong from a developed moral sense. Long, in-depth conversations that dance from topic to topic are the order of the day. Discussions go deeper than cause and effect, tackling moral questions and analyzing motivations and applying them to their lives. Ask leading questions and make your child work through ethical issues. Make them see the weaknesses in both sides of the argument and determine who is right, who is wrong and why. They can read great books on world civilizations and understand them now. Let them study the development of human thought. They exit this stage ready to apply facts, rules and morals to life's situations.

Questions to Ponder

1) What stage(s) does your child(ren) fall into?

2) What is the goal in the Logic Stage?

Chapter 11
Discipline (How do I Spank?)

Instruction & discipline are more about the training of the heart of the parent, than the heart of the child. The child only knows what you teach her. If from day one you are moving with purpose and consistency, your child will know what is expected of her and there will be little conflict of wills.

Why Don't I Just Talk to my Child?

Discipline is training in being self-controlled and alert.

> *Be sober-minded; be watchful. Your adversary the devil prowls around like a roaring lion, seeking someone to devour.*
> 1 Peter 5:8

Reasoning does not form "self-controlled and alert". Self-controlled and alert are trained and taught. When you reason with your child you are trying to get them to see and agree with your understanding of their actions and the consequences. The problem is, the ability to reason well is developed in a child in the early teen years, this is why we teach elementary students multiplication tables as facts to be memorized, spelling is taught as rules and the alphabet is as a song. Don't try to reason with your young child to get them to want to do good deeds. God tells the child to love and obey Him by loving and obeying their parents. Tell them how to act and train them to act that way, and use discipline if they are reluctant learners. If they choose to not do what God directs them to do.

At the writing of this book, popular culture is moving toward the philosophy of no discipline for wrong actions. When correction occurs it takes the form of reasoning, encouragement, or correction of the adult's actions rather than the child's. This is the new discipline. But God does not discipline us this way. By His word in Hebrews, He disciplines us for our good so that we can share in His holiness. His discipline is painful, not pleasant and it brings about the peaceful fruit of righteousness to those who are trained by it.

> *... he disciplines us for our good, that we may share his holiness. For the moment all discipline seems painful rather than pleasant, but later it yields the peaceful fruit of righteousness to those who have been trained by it.*
> *Hebrews 12:10-11*

The Umbrella

Let me paint a picture. Imagine a protective covering of God, like an umbrella. When we sin we step out of that protective covering and our relationship with God is splintered. Discipline restores our relationship and brings us back under God's protective covering. We must remember that our actions do not determine our standing before God. Jesus's death and resurrection alone did that. Our sin breaks our relationship with God, it puts a wall between us and God,

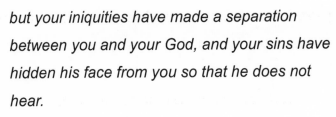

> *but your iniquities have made a separation between you and your God, and your sins have hidden his face from you so that he does not hear.*
> Isaiah 59:2

Discipline draws us back in and helps restore the intimacy. This is what is meant in Hebrews 12 when the Bible says those who are trained by discipline receive the peaceful fruit of righteousness.

Discipline is NEVER to be Given out of Anger but a Pure & Sincere Desire for the Child's Best

We discipline for clearly defined reasons. We don't discipline out of anger or frustration. The discipline and the consequences must be clearly defined beforehand. We don't discipline randomly. We discipline to impact the heart, character, safety and conduct. Our goal is godliness.

Clearly discussed expectations and consequences will keep you as a parent from frustration. You must have as your motivation for discipline to bring your child back into right relationship with God. If you are angry you have lost perspective. Have you ever wondered why you raise your voice to your children? We raise our voice to our children because we feel helpless, we feel that there is nothing we can do so we yell and hope our child obeys our previous instruction if it is louder. As you learn this process of discipline and spanking, you will no longer feel helpless. You will no longer get frustrated because you will know what to do. Your child will know what you are to do. You can spank with a calm demeanor because this is the consequence to their action. You do this because we as parents must obey God also. God said we must not spare the rod or we will spoil the child. We must train unto righteousness so that they will not depart from the path God has for them.

Have you ever seen a judge pronounce a sentence because he was angry or frustrated? This doesn't happen often because a judge's discipline is the follow through of predetermined consequences to actions. If it were personal, the judge would step down and allow another judge to preside the case. This is because discipline is never to be a knee-jerk reaction out of anger or frustration.

When do You Spank?

We spank for only a handful of offenses, and these are identified beforehand with the child.

Example: Lying

Lying is a big one in our home because it is a big one in the eyes of God. God says that all lies come from the father of lies, the Devil, and when you lie you are treating the Devil as if he is your father and you are acting like him.

You are of your father the devil, and your will is to do your father's desires. He was a murderer

> *from the beginning, and does not stand in the*
> *truth, because there is no truth in him. When he*
> *lies, he speaks out of his own character, for he is*
> *a liar and the father of lies.*
> *John 8:44*

The Bible says Jesus is the truth and the truth sets us free. It is important that our children see their sinful actions as sin and know the spiritual significance. We don't discipline for random reasons, we discipline for godliness. We discipline so that relationships are restored and God is honored.

In our home lying is a big offense and receives 4 swats to the bottom. All others receive 3 to 5. The first time our child lies we explain the truths of John 8 and lead them to understanding of their sin, and lead them through repentance and prayer. We then explain that if they lie again, they will receive 4 spankings for lying. We explain that this is a training time and they will get one more training time before the spanking consequence begins. We tell them that we will spank them because we love them so much that we will not let them destroy themselves and their relationship with their God and creator. He created them for a purpose and though it is our honor to join Him in the work He is doing in their life, it is hard, and sometimes we both end up in tears.

For example, let's say the next offense was subtle deception. We explain to them that this too is lying. You may not have said anything that is untrue but you knowingly mislead someone to believe something that is not true. We have them explain to us what will happen next time they lie and why. Then we have them pray through repentance.

The next offense we calmly remove them to a private place and talk to them about their lie. We have them explain to us the consequence of lying. We then train them through this process. They pull down their pants. The general rule is if you can be in the room when they dress and shower then they pull down their own pants revealing naked bottom. If they shower in private, they keep their pants or underwear up. Have them bend over and using a paddle, a 10 gallon paint stir stick works well, spank them on the bottom 4 times. Each swat should hurt. You are doing this so that you will never have to do it again.

A few things to note. Spank the bottom only. Never use your hand if they are out of the toddler stage. This is a calm, under control, pre-planned situation. No yelling, no anger, no arguing, no chasing the child or having them run around, no physical restraints. The child is to know when it starts and when it ends, 4 swats and it is done.

After the last swat, scoop the crying child into your lap and tell them that sin breaks our relationship with God, but you love them and God loves them more. He forgives our sin and restores our relationship when we repent. Just like spanking is our consequence for lying, there is a big consequence for sin. Jesus came so He could take your consequence for sin. God loves you so much, don't you want to love Him back? When you lie you are not loving God. But sometimes you are tempted to lie aren't you? You know what Jesus did for you? He sent the Holy Spirit to help you with strength to be able to not lie. Do you see why you need Jesus every day? Let's pray and tell God that you are sorry for lying because it is disobeying Him, and ask Him to help you not lie ever again.

Every spanking session ends with your child praying for repentance and you praying for your child and the Christ-like character being formed in him, and of course, a big hug. When our children emerge from the room after a spanking they are usually smiling and happy. The consequence is over, the sin is forgiven, the relationship with parents and with God is restored and there is no more judgement or condemnation for what they have done. The weight of sin has been lifted.

The last thing to do is, if their sin affected another person, they must go and apologize. An apology has 3 parts: say I'm sorry, name the sin, give the person a hug. This is the first thing that they must do after walking out of the room.

A few more things to note. Spanking is done in private. It is not your goal to embarrass your child but to restore him. Initially you may need to have your child repeat after you a prayer of repentance, but ultimately they must grow to seek forgiveness through prayer on their own and learn the words to use in this process.

There you have it. If you train your children well to know your authority, to know that their life is to bring glory to God, to know their worth in Christ, to know safety and freedom in the structure of their day, to know your love is for them, and if you are consistent, you will only need to spank your child 5 to 10 times in their lifetime. By the way, the earlier you start spanking your child, the fewer spankings they will need.

At What Age do You Begin Spanking?

Once your child begins disobeying or rebelling or showing signs of resisting your instruction, it is time to spank. If your child starts arching their back, flailing the legs and screaming, they need to know a spanking. At this young stage a spanking just consists of your hand on the fatty part of their thigh, quick and firm a couple of times. Follow this with simple instructions, "Don't do that. Sit up straight when mommy is holding you. Don't pull away." Tell them what not to do and what to do.

Some of the things we spank for:
Direct rebellion or disobedience to our word
Lying and deception
Unkindness to others, especially siblings

Once my children were in a group of other children playing and they did not respond when I called. This was our first incident of selective hearing. I explained to my children that from this point forward, they must hear my voice. If they did not hear my voice they would be disciplined with 3 spankings. We all have the ability to hear familiar sounds, even when there is noise all around us, even when others do not notice that particular sound. As parents, we alone look out for the safety of our children like no other. If a situation were to arise where my children were in danger and I could only reach them with my voice, they must hear me and obey immediately, without question. If I say, "Don't move!" because they are about to walk into a spider web or in front of a moving car, they must hear and obey without question. More importantly, this skill of selective hearing reflects in their relationship with God. They must hear His voice no matter how loud the busyness of life becomes. Their hearing must be selective even if others don't hear His voice. By the way, my children never used "we didn't hear you" as an excuse again. They made it a point to hear me.

Suffice it to say, there will be things unique to your family that you will need to make areas of discipline. Before spanking your child for an offense, make it clear to them what the offense is, what the correct action is and what the discipline will be. Take the time to train them before implementing spankings.

A side note: Spanking is part of training the child. The key factor is training, not spanking. I was with a parent recently who went to put her young child into a high chair to eat. The child did not want to be put down and squirmed, cried and flexed her legs to prevent being put into the chair. The mom ultimately gave in and continued holding the child. This mom has trained her child and the child now knows what to do if she does not want to be put down. The child has learned what actions will bring about the desired reaction, and the mom, without knowing it, has trained her child.

Knowingly or not, you are training your child. Be aware of the things that you are responding to and know that you are reinforcing behavior. Do not do things because your child cries, whines, or complains unless you want your child to always cry, whine, and complain when they want their way. If your child cries and complains make sure there is not a real problem like a dirty diaper, or pinched thigh, or hunger. If there is no problem, tell the child they are fine and they need to stop crying, then go about doing what you intended and teach the child that crying and whining does not get your way. Sometimes you will need to let them cry until they learn this lesson.

Please know that discipline is NOT your main source of training. Most of your training and instruction will be direct and intentional, it will not be a response to bad behavior, but proactive teaching of how a child should act. The better you proactively train your child the less you will need to discipline them.

Bible verses on this topic from the Amplified Bible.

> *Discipline and teach your son while there is hope, and do not [indulge your anger or resentment by imposing inappropriate punishment nor] desire his destruction.*

Discipline

Proverbs 19:18

Foolishness is bound up in the heart of a child;
the rod of discipline [correction administered with
godly wisdom and lovingkindness] will remove it
far from him.
Proverbs 22:15

Do not withhold discipline from the child; if you
swat him with a reed-like rod [applied with godly
wisdom], he will not die.
Proverbs 23:13

The rod and reproof (godly instruction) give
wisdom, but a child who gets his own way brings
shame to his mother. Correct your son, and he will
give you comfort; yes, he will delight your soul.
Proverbs 29:15, 17

He who withholds the rod [of discipline] hates his
son, but he who loves him disciplines and trains
him diligently and appropriately [with wisdom and
love]

Purposeful Parenting

 Proverbs 13:24

Questions to Ponder

1) What do those trained by discipline receive?

2) What is to be your motivation in disciplining your child?

3) What are a few things we spank for?

"The obedience and service of God's people will glorify Him most when they consciously and manifestly depend on His help; and His grace to do what they do."
- John Piper

Question/Answer: My Child is a Hitter

"With the swatting it really breaks my heart and sometimes I'm left wondering why am I spanking this person for hitting me? Am I not doing the same thing I'm telling her not to do? When I spank her leg or hand it turns red but she still keeps doing what I tell her not to do. She cries and will still hit me or play in the dog's water bowl. I just don't know how hard I'm supposed to spank her."

You are definitely NOT the first to ask this question. It makes me smile. You are not the only one to ever come to this place. It's a good question.

There definitely is a difference between "hitting" and "spanking". Remember when I said NEVER to spank from a place of anger or frustration? Well, when someone hits another, it's usually out of frustration.

Frustration occurs when something comes between you and your goal. Anger is frustration out of control. A person can be frustrated and not yet out of control.

When a person acts out in anger they have stepped into sin. When Liesl hits you, her frustration is out of control. She wants what she wants. She's upset because you got between her and her goal. She is frustrated. She then attempts to get back to what she wants to accomplish, i.e. splashing the water in the dog bowl, if once again you don't allow her, and tell her "don't" (that's my word of preference over the word "no") and she responds by hitting you, you then take hold of both her hands in yours, firmly yet gently. You look her in her eyes and with sincere love AND firmness of voice you say, "Don't do that! You don't hit mommy. Ever!" That's the instruction session. There always has to be an instructional session. You can't discipline for something you never taught them. Now she has the instruction. She has been told/instructed in what is expected of her. Oftentimes parents expect an action from their child without telling/teaching them what that action should be. This instruction session should be done eye to eye. Preferably, you come down to her eye level. If she is still not responsive, then it's time for a couple slaps on the back of the hand or on the thigh. As she gets bigger it might have to progress to diaper-off-bottom swats. These are always followed up with more instruction, prayer, kisses and hugs in the midst of her crying. If she continues to hit at you, throw a tantrum or yell, you will repeat the above, (prior to the prayer part) but will take her and place her in her crib. You must be consistent in this. She must understand that this is the way we/you as a family function.

Once again, your heart's attitude will come through in the disciplining of your daughter. She will be able to tell the difference between hitting and spanking. Your loving correction should never be confused with you "hitting" her. Your love and concern for her heart and well-being should so permeate her spirit that she knows instinctively that you mean nothing but good for her.

Before I answer the question regarding how hard to spank, I must tell you that no loving parent escapes a broken heart over having to spank their child. Spanking is a hard thing to do. It takes strength to obey God and spank our children. That strength is born out of love. How hard you spank depends on the child. Is she reacting from the sting of the swat or is she just responding from frustration? You will have to gauge it by her response. A spanking must be painful in the moment. The truth of the matter is, if you have won the heart of your child, she will be heart broken by the fact that her beloved mommy had to spank her. Even a soft swat will bring her to heart felt tears.

Win her heart. Let her know you are for her good, even if it means keeping her from what will be bad for her. No matter how badly she wants it. She has to know you will fight for her good in any and every situation, even if it means fighting her for HER good.

Question/Answer: My Child is Aggressive

"Hi Melissa, my mom said I should ask you what you did when your kids were aggressive or hit. Albert has been in a hitting phase for a while. He has gotten better but is still being too aggressive with other kids. Today he threw sand in a girl's eye at the park. We have done timeouts every time. We used to spank but have not been doing that much anymore. Instead of spanking, we are trying to have him redo what is kind. We think part of the problem was that he was not in daycare or around kids much and not using his words, though Charles did take him to the park every day. This year I take him to the park and to day care at the gym and church several times a week. I think half the time it seems like he is aggressive if a kid takes his toy, but lately it just seems like he is experimenting with how rough he can be. I don't know what to do. A couple times I have done whatever he did back to him, like pushing his

head, but I don't want to throw sand in his face and I don't like the idea of 'see this is how it feels' because it focuses on unkindness. This is why we aren't spanking as much. Unless he does a very harsh painful thing or dangerous thing to his sister, like pinching her. He has not done anything like that for several months now. I think part of it is being a boy and also being an only child up until now. I am home now and we aren't going to do daycare or preschool or else that would help. I am exhausted and feel like no one likes him and that I must not be disciplining him. I know I need to not think that but it's hard. Charles and I are more watchful and react to everything, more than most other parents, and yet Albert is worse than other kids. Thanks for any help you can give."

Hello Caroline. I am sorry to hear that your little Albert is struggling so, but be encouraged, as you train him and discipline him, he will learn how to behave, and more importantly at this stage, how not to behave.

Question/Answer

Jonathan and I experimented once with the whole NO
SPANKING philosophy. It just doesn't work, Caroline!
Each child is different and does respond differently.
One will need more spanking than another. Some
children, like our Elyona, are hurt at just the thought of
having upset us in any way. We were never ones to
yell at our children, but just a stern word was enough
to bring Elyona to tears. Overall, there is a reason
scripture says if we spare the rod, we will spoil the
child. Our child was spinning out of control and the
"no spanking" experiment was a source of propelling
him further out of control.

Once we began being clear in our expectations, clear
regarding the consequences for lack of his
compliance to these expectations, and we were
diligent to follow through on our word, things began to
change quickly. Yes, he was defiant! Although not
directly to us. None of our children have ever been
directly defiant to us. But he became resistant to any
other authority. I think your mom had to spank him
once. We had to give authority, to those we trusted, to
spank him in our absence. Things had gotten so far

out of control that all lines crossed had to be attended to immediately, he had to understand that we "said what we meant, and meant what we said." During this season, only your mom or Cindy babysat for us. If they couldn't, we didn't go. This was "intervention" at its best.

As to timeouts, there are several inherent flaws in timeouts that make it a poor instrument for deterring bad behavior. You have to read Hebrews 12 to get a basic understanding of how discipline works and what it accomplishes. I will summarize it but you should read it.

- God disciplines us and we discipline our children because of the sin struggle, verse 4.

- Discipline is an act of love, not anger or frustration, it is not unkind, verse 6 and 8.

- We should subject ourselves to loving discipline and respect the discipliner, verse 9.

- Discipline is for our good and to make us godly, verse10.

- Discipline must be painful, not pleasant, verse 11.

- Discipline is a training tool that develops right living, verse 11.

- Discipline is to lead us to repentance and restore intimacy of relationship, verse 17.

Timeouts do not accomplish many of these requirements of discipline and therefore are not good tools to end bad behavior and motivate good behavior. Making your child redo what is kind is equally as ineffective because it removes consequences for bad behavior. I do say that I agree with you about not doing to him what he has done to others. We don't want to address our parenting in this way. It reduces it to pettiness. That isn't what we want to do. We want to exalt our children's thinking and actions to the heights the Lord has called them to. We need to be continuously reminding our children, from the beginning, whose they are and what they are called to. God has loved us through Jesus and because He loved us, we love others. So as you diligently and faithfully spank him/them, to the glory of God, remind them of this fact. We love because we are loved by God. When he acts out and hits someone, throws sand on them or even speaks unkind words, he isn't walking in the love of Jesus. You must guide his heart to the One who shepherd's our hearts, Jesus.

Caroline, your son is not aggressive because he is a boy, only child and not in daycare. These things do not make a child aggressive or bring out aggressiveness in a child. Your child's aggressive behavior is an outward display of a condition of the heart. Your son has a heart need that is not being met and he is unable to communicate that need verbally. This develops a frustration that shows itself as aggression. You need to find out what his heart is crying out for and meet his need.

My observation in general is that most children that are aggressive have an unmet desire for a soul connection with their parents. Their parents are intellectually and physically involved with the child but not engaging with the child on a heart level. To engage your child on a heart level requires a perspective change. You would need to pray for and desire to engage your child on a heart level. This involves seeing your child as a joy to be around and someone you want to spend time with, and not seeing them as a burden, or a bother, or as something to accomplish on the list of things to do. This involves spending quality time together like reading a book or doing projects together.

I hope this helps. Just remember that the goal is to focus his heart on Jesus. His heart needs Jesus. Help him to see his need and teach him to go to and trust Jesus. Teach him to go to Jesus and repent and seek forgiveness. Teach him to love Jesus. Teach him to know that Jesus has the power he needs to obey and do the things that are pleasing to Jesus.

Question/Answer: My Child is Strong Willed

"What would be a good study or book on biblical parenting during these early years? Also, I need help with navigating obedience with Denise. Some days are better than others. She is strong willed and has a hard time obeying even if I swat her hand, thigh, or redirect her. It's a little defeating some days and I just don't know what to do."

Good to hear from you, Claire! We love and miss you a bunch!

First off, perspective! The strong willed child is a gift from the Lord. How you view her and how you view your responsibility toward her will make a difference in how she responds to you. It's mostly an unseen thing, but somehow, I'm sure it's the spirit of God, children pick up on what we think of them.

Secondly, parenting is more about training yourself than the child. What is it you desire to see in her? Are you yourself responding in this way?

Question/Answer

It is said that more is caught than taught. I agree! Usually children do what they see rather than what they are told. You can talk from sunup to sundown, but if what you are doing (demonstrating) day to day doesn't match what you are saying (telling her, training her, requiring of her) she will most naturally do what you do instead of what you say!

So, for example, if you are teaching her to respect you, (because that's where obedience comes from, right? It comes out of respect motivated by love), then she must see you demonstrating respect to her daddy, and vice versa. This is just a small start, but it reaps a great big harvest, one that will continue into her teen years and adulthood.

The last thing is prayer. Everything having to do with parenting, and all of life, must be preceded by, followed up with, and continued in MUCH MUCH prayer.

One more thing in regards to respect and obedience. Many young parents in our current culture desire to raise independent thinkers. I think raising children to become independent thinkers is awesome. But independent from whom? Hopefully from this world system, while being fully dependent on God and His ways. This is done by first teaching children to be submissive to the will of their parents. A child's ability to reason well does not develop until the middle school age, and it does not develop well without you training it. Even when it has been developed, it does not trump common respect for the dignity of any individual, especially mom & dad. You do not develop independent thinkers by letting a child determine and do whatever they want. This develops disobedient, disrespectful children who consider their needs above all others and expect others to do the same.

As far as books go, "Shepherding a Child's Heart" by Ted Tripp gets my vote. The heart of the child is of most importance. This book will help you learn to tend your child's heart as God intends.

By the way, if you are motivated by true love, 1 Corinthians 13 type of love, then you should continue with the discipline. If it gets no response, the slap on the back of the hand or thigh must not be stinging enough to create a reaction for her. Unfortunately if it doesn't sting a bit, it doesn't have an effect. Again, your heart must be in the right place to be able to discipline effectively in love. NEVER, NEVER, NEVER physically discipline your child if you are angry.

The act of spanking is a method of disciplining a child that must be motivated out of a passion for good toward that child, not out of pride to be obeyed. You must have a conviction that God's ways and God's will is best for your life, as well as the life of your child.

I am blessed by being able to come alongside you and your family.

Appendix

Life

One of the things Jesus said about himself is that he is the life. Jesus offers life to all who receive him. This is not just existence but an abundance of life. The Bible says,

> *Whoever has the Son has life; whoever does not have the Son of God does not have life.*
> *1 John 5:12*

This life includes the forgiveness of sins, eternal life in heaven and Jesus involved in your life on earth. This is a fulfilled life. If you want to know and live life in Jesus you simply go to Jesus and trust him for it.

If you believe and pray this prayer Jesus will give you new life in him.

Jesus, I know that I am a sinner and I know that I can't save myself. But you have offered me a gift of life if I would just believe in you as the one who takes away my sin and gives life. So I give you my sin because I believe you died as my substitute, and I receive now the life that you promised. Thank you for my salvation. In Jesus name, amen.

If you believe on Jesus, he has forgiven your sins and given you life. Congratulations and welcome to the family of God. The bible says:

But to all who did receive him, who believed in his name, he gave the right to become children of God.
John 1:12

What Now?

Tell your pastor or a Christian friend that you are a newborn believer. They will help you grow and encourage you in your new faith. Find a church that teaches the Bible, join with them on this journey of life. Join a Bible study and learn to study God's ways. Mostly, fall in love with God.

Bibliography

All biblical references are NIV unless otherwise acknowledged

Oganowski, Kristen (2017). 10 Dark Parenting Truths We Never Talk About. Retrieved from https://mom.com/baby/45996-10-dark-parenting-truths-we-never-talk-about/

Blackaby, Henry; Blackaby, Richard; King, Claude (2007). Experiencing God

Bauer, Susan Wise; Wise, Jessie (1999). The Well-Trained Mind: A Guide to Classical Education at Home

Made in the USA
Middletown, DE
22 June 2021